# THE Lost Art
## OF
# Room
# Travel

Jennifer Barrett

# THE Lost Art
## OF
# Room
# Travel

Published by Koala Cove Press
PO Box 3109, Kingsley, 6026
Western Australia
Australia
First published in Australia by Koala Cove Press 2013

Copyright © Jennifer Barrett 2013

Jennifer Barrett asserts the moral right
to be identified as the author of this work.
All rights reserved. No part of this publication may be reproduced,
stored in a retrieval system, or transmitted, in any form or by any
means, without the prior written permission of the copyright owner.

Cover photos © Wendy Barrett
Cover design and typesetting: Heather Leane, Sunbeam Books


National Library of Australia
Cataloguing-in-Publication entry:

Author: Barrett, Jennifer K.
Title: The lost art of room travel / by Jennifer Barrett

ISBN:   978 0 9875965 0 5 (paperback)

Subjects: Books and reading,
Imagination, Travel, Nostalgia, Memory,
Western Australia – social conditions
Dewey Number: 028.9

*For Ben*

# CONTENTS

# INTRODUCTION

*"Books are the treasured wealth of the world and the fit inheritance of generations and nations."* - Henry David Thoreau

Once upon a very different time, an illegal duel was fought between a young Frenchman and his opponent. The results of this skirmish and its subsequent events have continued to echo through the generations for more than 200 years.

The year was 1790 and the French combatant was 27 year old Xavier De Maistre. Despite surviving the duel he did not escape entirely unscathed, as the Courts sentenced him to 42 days house arrest. During this enforced confinement De Maistre decided to explore an unusual travel destination, a room within his own apartment, in the city of Turin. De Maistre wrote about his journey and, as he put it, a new mode of travelling was introduced to the world. De Maistre's book, titled "A Journey Round My Room", was a success from the moment it was first published in 1795.

By the time I bought a copy of the book in 2011, it had travelled across centuries to deliver its author's thoughts, emotions and experiences to my doorstep. Luckily for me, at some point in its journey, it had helpfully been translated from the French in which it was originally penned.

Books embark on a perilous odyssey when they are launched into the world and into the tides of Time. Initial high regard for its worth won't necessarily save a tome from becoming irrevocably lost somewhere en route to the future. It is serendipitous for his successive generations of readers that De Maistre's book has so far managed to successfully navigate across the years. I, and the countless other readers of De Maistre's work would have been only the shadowy, as-yet unborn people of the future to him.

In 1798 De Maistre set off on a second journey around his room, this time at night, and titled the resulting account "A Nocturnal Expedition Round My Room." De Maistre's travelling may have been physically restricted to the confined space within the walls, but his imagination heeded no such constraints, resulting in observations that were much more than simply descriptions of a room.

De Maistre refers to the power of imagination when he comments on the legal system which sentenced him to house arrest:

*"They have forbidden me to go at large in a city, a mere speck, and have left open to me the whole universe, in which immensity and eternity obey me." (A Journey Round My Room, p. 150)*

De Maistre's unconventional and entertaining approach to travel has inspired me to attempt to follow in his footsteps, as others have done over the years. Instead of journeying around a bedroom as he did, I will explore my study, which although small is hopefully interesting enough to justify being a "travel destination". As De Maistre said so eloquently, the whole universe is open to us if we are willing to use our imaginations.

De Maistre said that long before his house arrest he had planned to one day journey around his room. His enforced confinement merely gave him the opportunity to begin it sooner than he originally intended. My situation is very different, not being confined to my room for duelling – or anything else for that matter. Chronic ill-health for the past two years has, however, meant that I spend most of my time at home, sometimes not leaving it for a week or more.

Until I read De Maistre's books the idea of a journey that didn't require the traveller to even step outside had never come close to entering my mind. Now however, it seems the logical travel choice for me, and I am keen to discover whether I can turn the disadvantage of limited freedom into a positive, as De Maistre did.

Although I am walking in De Maistre's footsteps regarding his unusual style of travel, my journey will be vastly different to his. Our locations, both historically and geographically, are worlds apart, as are our personal circumstances and experiences. These factors will all ensure that our respective travel tales follow very divergent paths.

Because my journey has been inspired by De Maistre's stories, my narrative will be interspersed with excerpts from his first book "A Journey Round My Room." Each of these passages will be clearly marked as being De Maistre's words, to avoid any uncertainty regarding authorship.

De Maistre's books were originally written and published in French. Since then there have been a number of English translations made at various times, by different translators. I have used an English language edition of "A Journey Round My Room" which was translated by Henry Atwell and first published in 1871, by Hurd and Houghton, New York.

Before beginning my own journey it seems fitting to first hear from De Maistre as he sets off on his travels:

*"I shall traverse my room up and down and across, without rule or plan. I shall even ziz-zag about, following, if needs be, every possible geometrical line. I am no admirer of people who are such masters of their very step and every idea that they can say: 'Tomorrow I shall make three calls, write four letters, and finish this or that work'. So open is my soul to all sorts of ideas, tastes, and feelings; so greedily does it absorb whatever comes*

*first, that....but why should it deny itself the delights that are scattered along life's hard path? So few and far between are they, that it would indeed be senseless not to stop, and even turn aside, to gather such as are placed within our reach. Of these joys, none, to my thinking, is more attractive than following the course of one's fancies as a hunter follows his game, without pretending to keep to any set route. Hence, when I travel in my room, I seldom keep to a straight line. From my table I go towards a picture which is placed in a corner; thence I set out in an oblique direction for the door; and then, although on starting I had intended to return to my table, yet, if I chance to fall in with my arm-chair along the way, I at once, and most unceremoniously, take up my quarters therein. By the by, what a capital article of furniture an arm-chair is, and, above all, how convenient to a thoughtful man. In long winter evenings it is oftimes sweet, and always prudent, to stretch yourself therein, far from the bustle of crowded assemblies. A good fire, some books and pens; what safeguards these against ennui! And how pleasant, again, to forget books and pens in order to stir the fire, while giving one's self up to some agreeable meditation, or stringing together a few rhymes for the amusement of friends, as the hours glide by and fall into eternity, without making their sad passage felt."*

*(De Maistre, A Journey Round My Room, p. 11-13)*

# CHAPTER ONE

My bookcase, a relatively small specimen compared to many of its species, is the first stop on the journey around my study. It is only one of a number of bookcases dotted about the house, but this favourite holds many of my most-loved volumes. The shelves are full to over-flowing but the books refuse to stay confined for long. I often find that they have spilled out of their allotted spaces, wandered into other rooms and made themselves comfortable on sofas, side-cupboards and the kitchen table.

One of the most impressive of the many talents books have is their ability to double as miniature time-machines, transporting words and ideas to new readers even after their authors are long-dead, as De Maistre's did for him. Although other creative endeavours such as art, buildings and machines also successfully "travel" through time to the succeeding generations, for me books are the ultimate form of this, as their creators can pass along their exact thoughts through language.

Quite a large share of my bookcase has been claimed by a series of detective stories written by the Scottish author, Ian Rankin. Rankin's fictional detective, and leading man, is Inspector John Rebus. Although the Inspector has been allocated his fair share of frailties, the reader's sympathies are usually with him because his fears, dreams, short-comings and strengths are examples of the human condition. At times we can catch glimpses of ourselves in his journey. Rebus comes to life as a realistic, flawed character, but one who at his core is a man with a strong moral compass. Despite him often writing his own rules as he goes, there is never really any doubt which side he is on.

For me, detective stories are only partly about seeing the crime solved and trying to work out who-dunnit along the way. They are also about watching the inter-play of characters as they juggle their personal and professional lives and how they deal with life in general. If the characters don't feel believable the story can't hold my interest.

Not only does Rankin succeed in bringing his people to life on the page, he is able to create a "sense of place" so strongly that I can almost feel the stabbing chill of a harsh winter wind, or the cobble stoned street underfoot. Rankin has made Edinburgh an important part of his Rebus series and it is a major character in its own right. Inspector Rebus and his city have become so inextricably linked that there are walking tours of Edinburgh which visit locations featured in the books.

A few years ago I discovered that I didn't need a walking tour to visit Rebus's Edinburgh, the whole city became his. My son and I visited Edinburgh for a couple of days in 2005. To my surprise and delight, for the entire time we were there I had the surreal sensation of feeling as if I had been deposited into a Rebus novel. Everywhere we went I saw everything as if it was actually the world of Rebus and his colleagues. Life and Art had fused and I felt it was not beyond the realms of possibility to perhaps see Rebus wandering towards me, or catch a glimpse of him as he ducked into a pub. Rankin's stories were made into a T.V. series, starring John Hannah as Rebus. I didn't see the episodes but the front cover of one of my Rebus books "Black & Blue" (Orion, 2000) shows Hannah in his detective role. It is Hannah who I always picture as being Rebus and if he had, by some bizarre coincidence, crossed my path in Edinburgh it may have had me seriously questioning my sanity.

This rather novel (sorry, I just couldn't resist) experience was very enjoyable and an illustration of just how skilful Ian Rankin is in describing Edinburgh. It also demonstrates just how powerful good writing can be, blurring the boundaries between fact and fiction.

I once saw a notice pinned to a shelf full of teddy bears in a gift shop which confidently stated:

"Teddy bears are as real as you want them to be". This struck me as being very true, for children who pretend their teddies are alive, sharing their troubles and adventures with them, their toys are real. Children know on one level that their toys are actually only pieces of material and stuffing, but they choose to believe they are much more than this. In the world of their imaginations the teddies are as real as the children themselves. The imaginary may not have a physical reality as the "outer" world does, but it still exists in its own realm.

Well-written fiction that engages the imagination assumes a reality of sorts, just as the child's teddy bear does. Certain stories, particularly if they cross over from books to television or movies, capture the imaginations of millions of people. One example is J.K. Rowling's "Harry Potter" series, which became a world-wide phenomenon even before the movies were produced. For every one of her readers who avidly followed the adventures of Harry Potter and his friends, the world Rowling created was completely real in the non-physical sphere. The fact that these readers could discuss this world with each other, that others were experiencing the same imaginary reality, made it even more powerful. Key characters and scenes became part of the shared culture as if they physically existed or had actually happened.

Sometimes the boundaries of reality can become blurred, not by fiction but by actual events. In 2005 my son and I met up with my parents to spend a few days together in London at the end of our holiday in the U.K.

One morning we boarded an iconic red London bus to take us from our accommodation into the centre of the City. It was only a couple of months since the London terrorist attacks on the Underground and buses, so we all noticed when a few stops later a well-dressed man got on with a suitcase. He went upstairs onto the top deck, taking his luggage with him. We thought no more about it until he re-emerged a little later and got off the bus, with his case, a point we were careful to note.

The supposed rules of reality suddenly became questionable when a few stops later the same man with the same case was waiting to board the bus. There was no chance this was mistaken identity, as his thick curly blond hair was quite distinctive, as well as recognising his face, clothes and case. As our bus stopped he climbed on board, telling the driver he had inadvertently gotten off at the wrong place. My son hadn't seen him originally disembark, so was even more disbelieving as he had assumed he was still on board. Mum, Dad and I were incredulous as our bus had been travelling at a much faster than walking, or even running speed, and in a fairly straight line. There seemed to be no way in which this passenger could have got ahead of us, even without a sizeable suitcase to hamper him. I couldn't see whether the bus driver was surprised or not, but no-one else appeared to have noticed the incongruity. The four of us spent the rest of the journey delighting in this puzzle and trying to solve it, without success.

Later, on being told the tale, my sister offered a couple of light-hearted explanations, one being that the mysterious man was an alien on a fact-finding mission. He hadn't yet quite grasped the laws of physics on Earth so had not adjusted his behaviour accordingly. Alternatively he could have been a time-traveller from the future. When he re-boarded the bus he was on a return trip to our era but had re-entered at a time and place which jarred with his previous visit. I am quite happy to never know the truth, as the incident is now simply all part of the magic of London.

Most of us are fascinated by seemingly impossible events, which is why magic and magicians have remained popular, despite the ever-increasing entertainment options we have. A skilled magician can have his audience on the edges of their seats, and probably many of them wouldn't want to be told how the tricks actually worked. Young children often can't distinguish between what is possible and what's not, as they haven't yet had much experience in dealing with the natural rules of the world. Perhaps magic captures our imaginations because it returns us to this state of child-like wonder where there are no rules and anything can happen.

There are a number of detectives besides Rebus jostling for space in my bookcase, as one of my favourite fiction genres is Crime. One of these fictional detectives is Harry Bosch, who pursues justice for the people of Los Angeles, and the tales of his exploits take up a considerable amount of the shelving. Bosch is the creation of author Michael Connelly, who, like Rankin, is skilled at evoking a sense of place as well as creating complex and believable characters who come to life on the page.

As much as I enjoy the Rebus and Bosch books, which I have re-read a number of times, I found that I couldn't touch them during a period of very bad health in 2010. They were suddenly too realistic and I wanted to escape reality, not have more of it. This feeling probably developed because Perth seemed to be becoming increasingly violent. Almost every time I watched the news there had been a violent random attack on someone or yet another murder, sometimes in nearby suburbs.

When people are physically vulnerable due to illness, injury or age, it can sometimes make the world in general feel a much more intimidating place. Knowing you don't have the resources to either defend yourself or run away, you realise you are more at the mercy of others. Even knowing logically that the statistics are still against your becoming a victim, the fear remains. For people in this situation, who are often not very socially active, a lot of the information about what is happening in society is obtained through the media. Because the media often focuses on the sensational, violent and negative events, it is a very distorted view of reality. I am generalising wildly of course, many people who are physically vulnerable are still fearless, have active social lives, and would attempt to give as good as they got if attacked or threatened.

I needed something gentler than "police procedurals" to read, so turned to an old favourite, Agatha Christie. Miss Marple and Hercule Poirot fit my needs exactly with their "cosy mystery" style. There was still a murder to solve but it was so far removed from my everyday reality that it didn't feed my fears. The ingenious and often very complicated plots as well as the "olde-worlde" English ambience which Christie is so gifted at creating were also effective distractions. Due to my health issues I had no energy to do much other than read for awhile, so Miss Marple and Poirot really came to the rescue.

Books are wonderful companions for those too ill to do much, as they are happy to accompany their reader anywhere, from the sick-bed to a comfy armchair or wherever they are asked to go. Books don't get offended or hurt if their reader doesn't feel up to their company at times, or falls asleep while they're in the middle of recounting an entertaining anecdote. Gentle stories like those of Agatha Christie, where justice is always satisfied and problems are either solved or made manageable, are invaluable when reality seems too threatening and the reader needs to retreat into a simpler, safer world for awhile.

During this time I also re-discovered the Sherlock Holmes short stories by Arthur Conan Doyle. Although I had loved reading these in my teens, I wasn't sure if I would still enjoy them. Many books, movies, T.V. shows and music that we enjoyed when young don't travel well into our future years as our tastes and attitudes change, so it's always something of a relief when we discover one that has. Happily, the unique sleuthing methods of Mr Holmes were still a delight.

Another of my favourite authors, Alexander McCall Smith, came to my rescue during this time of needing placid stories to lose myself in. Like Ian Rankin, McCall Smith often paints his word pictures on the Edinburgh canvas. Unlike Rankin however, his stories explore the gentler, kinder side of the city, while still probing the inner reaches of his characters' psyches. McCall Smith has written a number of different series set in Edinburgh, none of them belonging to the crime genre. In an enchanting fusion of reality and fiction Ian Rankin actually pops up as a character in one of McCall Smith's books. Rankin's and McCall Smith's depictions of Edinburgh are in effect tales of two cities, each author illuminating different aspects of a multi-faceted metropolis.

The most wondrous aspect of books, whether fact or fiction, is that if we simply decipher the marks on their pages they will instantly transplant us into a different reality. When reading and identifying with one or more of the characters, a luxury not possible in real-life is that we get to enjoy the adventures without actually having to think of our own "lines" or plan the next move. It is all done for us. No actual person-to-person interaction is required, which allows even the most timid of readers to confidently engage in outlandishly heroic exploits.

Books don't give up their gifts without demanding some effort on our part. We need to use our imaginations to bring the scenes to life or the ink on the page will be virtually useless. The magic only truly happens when the author's words and the reader's imagination join together. Perhaps it is because of the effort required to read properly, that so many people don't, instead opting for the ease of television or movies.

Although stories classified as fiction are universally recognised as being inventions of their author's imaginations, to be successful they still need to stay connected to reality in certain ways. Readers of fiction agree to play the game of "let's pretend", but they still expect the characters, settings and events to appear realistic. This rule applies even for science-fiction and fantasy. Characters still need to behave in ways consistent with their own particular world. If they act illogically according to their own norms there has to be a reason for them doing so.

I remember abandoning a book in frustration when the main character began behaving and thinking in ways which didn't seem emotionally balanced. The author obviously didn't realise how badly wrong she had gotten it, because she wasn't trying to portray the character as mentally unstable. When characters behave or react in ways which make us think, "Hang on, they're not likely to do that", it destroys the illusion that we're reading about real people and the spell is broken.

When the author has a good understanding of the psychology of people and portrays the characters well it can be quite educational, particularly if it is dealing with situations of which we have no personal experience. The problem of course, is that unless the author has gotten it very wrong and our suspicions are aroused, we don't know when something outside our own experience or knowledge is inaccurate. Instead of increasing our awareness of how others feel and think, a writer who does portray his characters falsely but convincingly, whether intentionally or through ignorance, can sometimes cause considerable damage. Usually inaccuracies don't really matter much, but when significant issues are involved it is important not to create or perpetuate false information or stereotypes.

De Maistre talks about the pleasure he obtains from his books:

*"Our forty-two days will soon be ended; and even were it not so, a similar period would not suffice to complete the description of the rich country in which I travel so pleasantly.*

*My library, then, is composed of novels, if I must make the confession; of novels and a few choice poets. As if I had not troubles of my own, I share those of a thousand imaginary personages, and I feel them as acutely as my own. How many tears have I shed for that poor Clarissa, and for Charlotte's lover!*

*But if I go out of my way in search of unreal afflictions, I find in return, such virtue, kindness, and disinterestedness in this imaginary world as I have never yet found united in the real world around me. I meet with a woman after my heart's desire, free from whim, lightness and affectation. I say nothing about beauty; this I can leave to my imagination, and picture her faultlessly beautiful. And then, closing the book, which no longer keeps pace with my ideas, I take the fair one by the hand, and we travel together over a country a thousand times more delightful than Eden itself. What painter could represent the fairy land in which I have placed the goddess of my heart? What poet could ever describe the lively and manifold sensations I experience in those enchanted regions?*

*When I have had enough of tears and love, I turn to some poet, and set out again for a new world."*

*(De Maistre, A Journey Round My Room, p.109 - 112 )*

It would be interesting to know exactly which novels and poetry books De Maistre's library contained, and whether copies of any of them still exist in other people's bookshelves today. Perhaps some grace the libraries, established generations ago, of a few stately mansions. These long-lived libraries may also be the repositories of countless other forgotten works by long-dead authors, with numerous literary gems sitting quietly amongst the dusty tomes, patiently waiting to be re-discovered and launched onto a new generation of readers.

# CHAPTER TWO

On top of my bookcase is a collection of Magnum P.I. DVD's.

Last year (2011) I was beginning to go a little stir-crazy from rarely leaving the house and being too exhausted to do much of anything. My health status is very up and down and for a few months it was mostly down. I had even arrived at a point I thought could never be reached – I was no longer enjoying reading.

Although I had been managing to stay reasonably upbeat since beginning unpaid sick leave in April 2010, I began to feel mildly depressed, with occasional short-lived bouts of severe depression. I felt claustrophobic, confined to my house and garden for extended periods. Frankly, I was wallowing in a bit of "poor me" syndrome and knew I had to snap out of it. With a history of clinical depression I couldn't afford to let it get a claw hold in my head.

One day while searching the T.V. channels for something interesting, I found that a Magnum P.I. re-run was on, the first time I had seen an episode since they were originally aired in the 1980's. As I settled down to watch I thought it would probably be a bit cringe-worthy, as many television series from that era are when re-visited. Although I had been a huge fan of the Magnum episodes, I wasn't sure whether they would still hold the same appeal, decades later. However, somewhat to my surprise, I really enjoyed it. The episodes, which aired a few days a week, became something to look forward to. For the brief time it took Magnum and his friends to "save the day" I was transported away from the constricted confines of my house and deposited into the tropical beauty of Hawaii. The fact that the leading man, played by Tom Selleck, was very easy on the eye may have added to the show's attraction, but I admit nothing.

To avoid becoming victim to the fickle whims of television program schedulers who may cut the show adrift without warning, as they are apt to do, I soon secured my own supply of Magnum mood-enhancers. A combination of some daily visual escapism and using various previously learned mental strategies soon improved my mood and I was able to climb out of what had threatened to become a serious depression.

I had read to saturation point, so the books which were usually so good at providing me with a change of scene were temporarily ineffective. Magnum came along at just the right time, the different and visual medium of film being just what was needed. Often a holiday is an effective way to short-circuit the day-to-day routines and stresses of life. Sometimes even a couple of days away from our usual environment can be enough to re-charge the emotional batteries. Because of my situation I wasn't able to physically travel, but the DVD's allowed me to mentally live in Magnum World for a short while each day and happily that was enough.

Although occupying two vastly different fictional worlds, Magnum and Miss Marple are similar in some respects. Murderers and other miscreants are almost always brought to justice and the worlds of Magnum and Miss Marple are safe again, at least temporarily. Many of the Magnum episodes had a lot of humour in them, which was a good tonic.

Another reason the Magnum episodes appealed to me was that I had originally seen them when in my early twenties, so at a subconscious level I was connecting with my youth again while watching them. That's presumably why nostalgia is such big business, with re-runs of shows from the 70's, 80's and 90's, and clothing from previous decades coming back into vogue. People who were young when the originals made their debuts are reminded of their youth.

Apart from nostalgia for our own adolescence, we often miss the past in general, selectively remembering only the good parts, our memories happily co-operating by blanking out the unpleasant bits. We usually know that certain periods of our past are not the blissful utopias we sometimes choose to remember them as, but we do it anyway. Of course sometimes even a heavily censored memory can't override the sheer awfulness of certain past times for some people, and they would feel anything but nostalgic about them.

Perhaps we can often remember previous times as being better than they were because we don't feel all of the accompanying tensions and anxieties we had during that period. Day-to-day life throws up a constant stream of challenges both big and small, so most of us are rarely totally relaxed. When reminiscing however, all except the big challenges are conveniently forgotten, so if there were no major traumas we don't remember the same daily low-level stresses we face in the present. The past can use this advantage to good effect, letting us mistakenly believe life was simpler then.

Returning to the past via memory also has some of the same features as reading a book or watching a movie. There is no personal interaction required as the story has already been written, thus freeing us from the burdens of having to make decisions. Although at times, being able to change the past is exactly what we wish we could do.

Wandering down memory lane we can sometimes enter territory we haven't visited before, even though we may not realise it. Memory is very unreliable and not only can it conveniently forget certain things, it is also an expert at altering them. Sometimes this becomes obvious when two or more people are discussing a shared memory from their past. Their recollections may all be completely different, and at times even contradictory, but they can all visualise their own scenes and are convinced their version is the truth. Sometimes too, if we have been told stories or shown photos from our childhood, we can't tell if what we remember is the actual event or simply our imagination working off the later information.

When writing the piece about Magnum I checked the internet to see what years the show was produced. I was very surprised and a little disconcerted to discover that they had first been released in the United States in December 1980. This meant that a clear memory I have had for over thirty years is wrong. When I was travelling solo for the first time at eighteen I met a fellow youth hosteller on one of the islands on the Queensland Barrier Reef. For decades my memory has unblushingly told me that at the time, I thought this man bore a striking resemblance to Tom Selleck (Magnum). As this event happened before the Australian release of the show I could not possibly have thought such a thing. My memory had been lying to me. I now realise I probably thought the guy looked like Burt Reynolds, another famous American actor of the time. Somehow over the years the identity changed. (In my memory's defence, both of them sported impressive moustaches.)

Obviously this is a totally unimportant "false memory" in itself, but it demonstrates how easily and totally our memories secretly change on us while we're not looking.

The following passage is from the quill of De Maistre, as he talks about the joy and innocence of youth. I suspect his subconscious has done some serious censoring of his memory, as he paints a picture that is perhaps unrealistically idyllic:

*"What a wealth of delights has kind Nature given to those who can enjoy them. Who can count the innumerable phases they assume in different individuals, and at different periods of life! The confused remembrance of the pleasures of my boyhood sends a thrill through my heart. Shall I attempt to paint the joys of the youth whose soul glows with all the warmth of love, at an age when interest, ambition, hatred, and all the base passions that degrade and torment humanity are unknown to him, even by name?*

*During this age, too short, alas! The sun shines with a brightness it never displays in after-life; the air is then purer, the streams clearer and fresher, and nature has aspects, and the woods have paths, which in our riper age we never find again. O, what perfumes those flowers breathe! How delicious are those fruits! With what colours is the morning sky adorned! Men are all good, generous, kind-hearted; and women all lovely and faithful. On all sides we meet with cordiality, frankness, and unselfishness. Nature presents to us nothing but flowers, virtues and pleasures. The excitement of love, and the anticipation of happiness, do they not fill our hearts to the brim with emotions no less lively and various?*

*(De Maistre, A Journey Round My Room, p. 129 - 130)*

One of the few Australian books on my bookshelves is "My Brilliant Career" by Miles Franklin. Franklin was born in 1879 in New South Wales and this, her first novel, was published in 1901, to considerable acclaim. Being set in the 1890's the story's props, such as housing, transport and social conventions are naturally vastly different to our own, but the stage on which it is played out is easily recognisable, the Australian bush. Franklin's skill in describing the natural environment had me, at various points, breathing in the scent of the wattles, picturing paddocks full of grazing cows or feeling the crunch of the brittle, sun-dried stubble underfoot.

Although "My Brilliant Career" uses the bush as its setting, the story is actually about the suffering of a girl out of step with those around her. The main character longs for a different world than the one she feels trapped in. Franklin was only eighteen when she began writing her novel but already she had profound insights that would never have crossed the minds of many people twice her age.

The book was written at a time when the "bush" was a large and important part of Australian life. Most of the population lived in the countryside and everyone was heavily dependent on the food, wool and other materials it provided. It is very difficult, perhaps impossible, for a person to live in the bush without it affecting them. Whether they love it or hate it, the natural environment is not a blank page upon which people can simply write their stories. It will insist on being part of the narrative, whether through dramatic flourishes such as flood, fire or drought, or by calmly displaying its beauty and sharing its bounty. Because it is such a strong character it was inevitable that the bush would play a leading role in our early cultural identity. Australia's Aboriginals had been identifying with their land at a deeper level than most of the European settlers could ever imagine, for tens of thousands of years prior to this. Because the Australian bush can be a harsh and unforgiving place, people depended, sometimes for their lives, on their neighbours and companions, thus also developing the strong Australian "mate-ship" theme.

For a while the importance of the bush to the Australian identity remained strong even when people began migrating from the country areas into towns and cities. Even those who rarely ventured beyond the urban perimeters were still very conscious of the vast expanses of untamed land which lay just outside the glow of streetlights and neat rows of houses. Today most Australians live in cities and towns that hug the coastline, with the countryside becoming a holiday destination or perhaps just a vague idea. With air travel now so cheap and easy, many have little experience of just how immense our country is. Because of this, our national identity could not expect to remain focused on the bush, and it transformed into a new image to reflect the new way of life. The focus became the "sun-bronzed Aussie", fit and healthy and virtually living in the surf. Today this has changed again, with many of us seeing ourselves as a sporting nation, excelling at and being obsessed by athletic pursuits. Presumably this self-definition of our national character will also transfigure into something else sooner or later, as our interests and priorities alter over time. It will be interesting to see which direction it takes.

The next book I come across in my shelves is "This Side of Paradise", by F. Scott Fitzgerald, one of the most acclaimed American writers of the 20th century. This was Fitzgerald's first novel and although not as famous as his later tale "The Great Gatsby", it was greeted with considerable enthusiasm when it made its debut in 1920. "This Side of Paradise" is a coming-of-age story. It is a timeless tale of the struggle of young people to find their place in the world. Although the theme is universal, the story is set very firmly in the early years of 20th century America and offers an intriguing glimpse into a time and attitude far removed from our current experience.

As well as enjoying the ideas and themes that swirl and eddy throughout the book, I found that Fitzgerald's language is often a pleasure in itself. In one scene, the main character hopes to have a serious talk with a friend. He is very aware that time is short, as he has a train to catch:

*"..... train left at twelve-eighteen that night. His trunk and suitcase awaited him at the station; his watch was beginning to hang heavy in his pocket."*

After many adventures and misadventures, the main character, Amory, announces: *"I know myself, but that is all"*.

Amory was very fortunate to have achieved such self-awareness while still young. How many paths do we eagerly set off upon in our journey through Life, only to discover, partway along, that we are actually on one better suited to another type of traveller entirely? Until we know who we are, and recognise our core dreams, strengths and weaknesses, we cannot know which path is the one which is heading in the right direction for our particular needs. Some of us spend a large part of our lives stumbling over the obstacles in our chosen roads, continuously having to back-track and look for a new one before eventually, through good fortune or clearer vision, coming across the right path. I am very definitely in this group, and have accumulated quite a few "Frequent Flyer" points travelling in wrong directions in the past. That said however, sometimes a path can be perfect for our needs for part of the journey, but as we move further along it, we find we no longer wish to head in that direction and we need to consult our personal maps again.

Before leaving Fitzgerald and moving on, here is another sentence from his book, which I thought was rather beautifully expressed:

*"Then they turned out of the moonlight into the trellised darkness of a vine-hung pagoda, where there were scents so plaintive as to be nearly musical."*

Somewhere back in the mists of my teenage years I read a science fiction novel by Isaac Asimov, titled "The End of Eternity". While exploring the contents of my bookcase on this journey I began thinking about Asimov's book, and decided that my shelves were incomplete until a copy could be squeezed in somewhere between the current inhabitants. Despite the details being forgotten, with even the main themes now somewhat hazy, this story had remained as a special reading experience in my memories. Apparently "The End of Eternity" is considered by many to be one of Asimov's best works, and fortunately was still in print. The story plays with the concepts of Time and Reality, two subjects humanity has an enduring fascination with. In the hands of a Master like Asimov it was virtually destined that something special would be created that captured the imaginations of so many.

Reading it again, I discovered that as well as being very entertaining, there is a profound idea to the story. I had long-forgotten this aspect of the book but was delighted to find it, as it added to the richness of the reading experience. The concept is one which I have long believed, and which could be described as one of my philosophies of life, which made me start wondering... Since I first read this story sometime in my teens, a very impressionable age, did I perhaps integrate this idea into my life view and subsequently make decisions based on it? If I did do this, I owe Asimov a big "thank-you", because I feel my life has been the richer for it. I can't reveal what the "idea" was, because it would be a "spoiler" for Asimov's story.

I may be totally off-track in those particular speculations, but stories and books in general, whether fiction or non-fiction, can often help to create or influence a person's ideas or perceptions, for either good or bad. No single book can affect every one of its readers, but on the occasions when the author's words tune into something in the reader's psyche, powerful emotional changes can be set in motion. Perhaps the old saying "The pen is mightier than the sword" is accurate?

On top of the bookcase next to the DVD's is a small ceramic pot with a tiny Alexander Palm seedling, freshly sprouted and tentatively showing itself to the world. After becoming so absorbed in the make-believe world of Magnum and revelling in the lush tropical scenery of Hawaii, I decided to try growing a palm tree to bring a little of the tropical ambience into my study. The Alexander Palms are a native of Queensland but there are many expatriates happily growing in the Hawaiian Islands. They make good house pets until they get too big and need to be banished to the garden.

For the past couple of years I have had almost zero success with growing plants from cuttings or seeds, despite having many happy endings (or beginnings?) previously. Ever the optimist, I collected five seeds from a mature palm in my parents' garden, planted them and hoped for the best. The resident of the pot on my bookcase is one of two that have so far sprung into life.

At the moment this tiny seedling resembles a blade of grass and it will presumably be many months before its parentage could even be guessed at by a casual observer. It will be even longer before it begins its life's work of bringing a waft of lush tropical climes into its surroundings. This flaw in my leafy decorating plan is compensated for by the satisfaction I get from nurturing a plant from seedhood. The first sighting of a much anticipated shoot emerging from its earthy womb never fails to be a special moment for me. The longer the wait and the less the chance of success had been, the more satisfying it is. Because of this I am happy to enjoy my tiny palmlet's childhood, and the expectation that it will one day actually look like its older relatives is simply a bonus.

# CHAPTER THREE

My bookcase is by no means only home to works of fiction. I enjoy non-fiction just as much, both types of books satisfying different needs and moods at different times. Sometimes certain books come into our lives just when they will be of the greatest benefit to us.

An example of this is "The Element – how finding your passion changes everything", a book written by Ken Robinson, Ph.D. (with Lou Aronica). I happened merely by chance to catch the last part of a talk he was giving on television, where he was discussing his book. What I heard inspired me to immediately go on-line and purchase a copy. Robinson's book is about finding our true passion in life. I already knew that writing, and travel writing in particular, is my passion, but Robinson's words fuelled my enthusiasm even further. His book motivated me to actually commit to writing this "journey around my study" rather than just thinking about doing so. Robinson reminded me just how important following our life purpose is to our personal fulfilment and well-being.

I began reading Robinson's book a couple of weeks after turning fifty. As I seem to do every time I am pushed into a new decade, I had spent a few days playing hostess to a mini-crisis. Reaching the half-century seemed like a major milestone and I now felt closer to "old" than "middle-aged". I pulled myself together after a few angst-ridden days, partly by looking at the evidence that fifty is still a vibrant age. Many people are at the height of their careers at this point of their lives. To use two high-profile examples, America's President Barack Obama and Australia's Prime Minister

Julia Gillard both turned fifty in 2011. On a smaller stage, many people in senior management positions are fifty or older. I also remembered something I already knew but had lost sight of. Age is only a number and in many ways meaningless, because it is attitude that counts. Some people are born old, while others die young aged one hundred.

This reality-check reassured me that I was far from old, but I still couldn't shake the fear that I was too late to seriously explore a new life path. Reading Robinson's "The Element" banished my doubts and fears, as he gives examples of people who have made major changes in direction in later life and have never looked back. Although obviously not all dreams are attainable at later ages, many are. Robinson assures us that some ventures even benefit from maturity. This was exactly what I needed to hear.

I had serendipitously found De Maistre's "A Journey Round My Room" while wandering around the Book Depository website a few months prior to this. My own journey around my study would never have begun if I hadn't discovered De Maistre's book. If I had come across it when my health was better I may not have had the patience to undertake a journey within a single room, so the timing was perfect.

Many people have similar experiences, of one or more books coming into their lives just when they are ready for them to make a profound difference in some way. It is yet another way in which books weave their magic, allowing an author to have a positive effect on a reader he has never met.

Travel narratives are another of my favourite reading genres. Bill Bryson is, for me, one of the top maestros of the field, combining keen observation of people and places with a very clever wit. I read Bryson's "Notes From A Small

Island" quite a few years ago and it was this book which first made me think that one day I would also write travel tales.

One of Bryson's books, titled: "Down Under" recounts his travels round Australia. In it he focuses quite heavily and very amusingly on the dangerous wildlife to be found here, and the various imaginative and unpleasant ways it can kill you. I recently happened across a television news article which I thought Bryson would have been delighted to see. It fit beautifully with his light-hearted theme of murderous fauna lurking behind every tree. It seems that in Australia, even on a golf course it is possible for the unwary to end up as lunch.

Carbook Golf Club, an 18-hole course in Brisbane, is believed to have the world's first shark infested water hazard. In the early 1990's the nearby Logan River burst its banks and flooded the golf course for an extended period of time. As the water gradually receded many fish of various species were left behind in the twenty-one hectare lake. Soon afterwards, the occasional sighting sparked a feeding frenzy of rumours that a shark was also now a resident of these fishy waters.

In recent years many people have seen them, with reports that there is often more than one shark. Video recordings have been made to back up these claims and there is no longer any doubt that this is one water hazard to which players are happy to donate their wayward golf balls permanently.

These unlikely inhabitants, measuring 2.4 to 3 metres long, have been identified as bull sharks. They are now welcome long-term residents of the golf-course, providing a fascinating talking point both within the club and outside of it.

Unlike many other countries, thankfully Australia has very few large predators. But unfortunately it makes up for its lack of man-eating mammals by accommodating many of the deadliest snakes on the planet. This abundance of homicidal reptiles sometimes makes life in summer a little fraught for card-carrying "snake-a-phobes" such as myself. Growing up in the country, on a few occasions I inadvertently came close enough to snakes to count their eyelashes. Certainly not a pleasant experience. Although these encounters would have immediately changed from terrifying to life-threatening if I had actually been bitten, prompt medical attention would have presumably been able to salvage the situation. It is a pity, and presumably the origin of my life-long phobia, that as a young child I overheard someone delightedly telling his companion about a type of snake so deadly that a bite would see you dispatched from the mortal coil within seconds. Although the teller of this tale was not referring to our local, slightly less poisonous varieties, the damage was done.

Last summer I realised my phobia was getting a little out of hand. This was despite now living in an urban environment, with the nearest tiny remnant of natural bush being a block or two away from my house. This location meant little however, as every year around the city there are a few reports of snakes taking road trips and ending up in someone's lounge-room, dog-kennel or similar presumably snake-proof sanctuary. Usually I am only slightly mindful of this remote possibility happening to me, but suddenly for no discernible reason my fears escalated. I knew I had to try and pull myself together when sticks began "hissing" at me. Every time I went outside into the garden and stepped on a dried twig or stick, the slight crackle noise it made from the impact transformed into a threatening hiss in my over-active imagination. I would then have to closely examine the source of such hostility to re-assure myself it didn't have fangs. Needless to say every stick, happily, has proved to be quite toothless – so far.

One type of travel narrative that has become very popular is that of an individual, couple or family re-locating to a different country, either temporarily or permanently. These tales often include amusing and sometimes horrifying anecdotes of cultural misunderstandings, the difficulties of foreign laws and government bureaucracies and domestic disasters. Interactions between the characters can often become almost larger-than-life due to the differences in culture and language, which add another dimension to the everyday social scene. This sub-set of travel tale is popular because so many people are fascinated by the idea of leaving their usual lives and beginning afresh in some exotic new location, whether short-term or forever. When we think about another place, perhaps a quiet village in France where many of these stories are located, we can't really believe that day-to-day existence could soon become as routine as it is at home. Our fantasies refuse to dwell on the fact that we can't escape the mundane chores of life however far we travel – we still have to shop for food, pay bills and wash our clothes. Inadvertently stepping into the excrement of a Parisian Poodle would be just as teeth-gnashing as stepping into that of a Perth pooch.

I suspect too that in these daydreams many people do a spot of re-inventing, imagining that in this new utopia they will be deluxe versions of themselves, confident, socially at ease with everyone and all of their anxieties and frustrations will have been left behind. (Or perhaps it's just me who does this?) The authors of these "relocating to a new environment" stories each have their own reasons for embarking on the adventure, and their own verdict as to how successful it was. For most of the authors I've read, their experiences have been very rewarding, enriching their lives despite considerable challenges along the way for some of them.

A handful of my books feature women on their own who travel to a number of different locations over the course of a year, hoping to re-discover themselves. These stories are examples of courageous women having adventures without needing the security of travelling companions, and often there is considerable personal growth by the end of the experience. These authors demonstrate what is possible, at any age.

I enjoy reading about life-altering travel tales because I am fascinated that a simple journey away from home and into a new environment can often have a profound effect on the traveller. Being in a new situation on one's own, with the connections to home responsibilities stretched thin by distance, experiences and observations are often more intense than usual. Without the familiar reference points which define our usual reality, we experience everything from a fresh perspective. Even our own personalities are no longer defined by those around us, as the people we meet on our travels are strangers with no personal experience of who we are. Sometimes when we've known people for many years it's not only their current personalities and behaviours we attach to them, but also those of their younger years. This can sometimes happen in families, where perhaps a child who was known for certain traits, such as irresponsibility or thoughtlessness, may always be seen this way to a certain extent by his relatives, even if his attitude is now quite different. Travel allows us to shed labels, whether they are accurate or not, and interact with the world from our current selves. It also gives us the chance to jettison the self-limiting beliefs we may have inflicted on ourselves. Being deposited onto a new stage without the props, scenery and scripts of our old lives to help or hinder us, we also have the chance to learn a lot about our own personalities by the way in which we deal with this new setting.

At the age of eighteen I travelled round Australia on my own for ten weeks, and this short period of time changed my life in unexpected and positive ways. I was extremely shy when I began my journey, barely able to speak to anyone I didn't know well, and with very little insight into either my own or other people's behaviour. I returned home with more awareness and, although still nowhere near being an extrovert, the seemingly impenetrable shell of my crippling shyness had been cracked open a little. In a new environment I had been the only one who knew I was shy, so had decided to try adjusting my self-belief. To my surprise I discovered that to a certain extent I could act as if I wasn't afraid. I still cowered on the inside but could project a relatively confident facade.

Just as books, people and circumstances can sometimes appear in our lives at just the right time when we can most benefit from them, so too can the journeys we take. I am convinced that the trip I took as a teenager was a determining event for the direction my life would head in. Many years later at the age of forty two I took a vacation in Brisbane, a week which proved to be unexpectedly life-changing. The clinical depression I had lived with for thirteen years disappeared during this time, and while the holiday itself wasn't the cause of my recovery it gave me the emotional space for it to happen. I will refer to what cured my depression a little later on. Although we don't expect the benefits of travel to always be so dramatic, each time we leave the familiarity of our usual environments the journey is full of potential adventures, and that is its irresistible attraction.

I can't leave the subject of travel before mentioning more about the author of "A Journey Round My Room", Xavier De Maistre. De Maistre engaged in a number of different careers throughout his long life. As a young man he was an officer in the Sardinian army. Later on he entered the Russian armed forces where he distinguished himself in the war against Persia and attained the rank of major-general.

De Maistre had wide-ranging interests, including a passion for painting, and gained a considerable reputation for his landscapes and miniature portraits. In addition to his two travel books, De Maistre wrote a number of other stories. As well as his creative endeavours he was also fascinated by the concept of flight. The first manned hot air balloon was launched in Paris in November 1783 and flew for 20 minutes. De Maistre decided he wanted to be part of this exciting new invention. On the 6th May 1784 he and a friend, Louis Brun, became the first people to fly above Savoy, piloting a hot-air balloon and managing to stay aloft for approximately 20 minutes.

Whenever I see a hang-glider effortlessly soaring through the sky I think what a pity it was for the countless generations who lived before the invention of manned flight. If they had but known it, they too could have felt the exhilaration of flying, as they already had the necessary materials. Unfortunately they tried to copy the birds by strapping "wings" to their arms and attempting to flap themselves airborne, with predictable results. If they had shifted their focus to the gliding facet of the bird's flying repertoire they would presumably have soon joined them in their sky-borne life-style.

Despite his adventurous and high-risk endeavours De Maistre managed to live to the ripe old age of 88 years, dying in his adopted country Russia in June 1852.

One of the other stories De Maistre wrote was "The Leper of the City of Aosta". It is a short story rather than a novel and as the title would suggest, is a rather grim tale. It is set in 1797 and is a dialogue between a leper and a military man who happened to be passing by. The leper has been banished from society and into a tower surrounded by gardens, where he has lived for the past fifteen years. Emotionally it wasn't an easy story to read, despite it being well-written, as the subject matter was distressing. Although this is a work of fiction it reflects the suffering of those unlucky enough to contract the awful, and at that time incurable, disease of leprosy.

De Maistre didn't create a miserable fate for his fictional character simply for the sake of stirring up our horror and sympathy. His leper, although lamenting his severe misfortune, also talked about the comfort and at times even happiness, he got from the simplicity of his lifestyle. The natural environment which surrounded him also provided considerable emotional sustenance. De Maistre's story is a tale of acceptance of one's circumstances, however dire. Perhaps he wrote it as a reminder to himself, as it would appear from his "room travel" stories that he sometimes struggled emotionally with the major and dangerous events occurring in his own life.

The following is a short but important passage, where the leper is explaining to his temporary companion:

*"In fine weather I spend whole days motionless on this rampart enjoying the fresh air, and the beauty of nature. At such times all my ideas are vague and indefinite; sadness rests in my heart without suppressing it; my eyes wander over that open country and the rocks that lie around us. These different aspects are so impressed upon my memory that they form, as it were,*

*a part of me, and each spot is a friend that I see every day with pleasure." (De Maistre, The Leper of the City of Aosta)*

Another genre of book which I have quite a few representatives of is the "how to write" category. These books have been wonderful teachers – the less competent ones having been evicted from my shelves and re-assigned to the charity bin long ago. As well as acquiring guidance in the writing craft, I find the act of reading these books makes creative ideas for my own stories come thick and fast.

One of the most important aspects of learning to write is to read voraciously, which allows the reader to unconsciously absorb vocabulary, sentence and story structure. Reading also teaches us how effective stories work and stimulates our imaginations. The fact that it helps us to write is only a bonus, because whether or not we ever put our own pen to paper reading is simply one of life's great pleasures. J.K. Rowling has done more than anyone else in recent history to open up the world of books to young people. By creating the Harry Potter series Rowling showed them that reading was exciting. She introduced them to a world of adventures and imagination beyond their computer games and television.

Even those children whose voluntary reading experiences began and ended with the Harry Potter stories have been exposed to the magic of books. Hopefully at some time later in their lives they will remember the delight they got from reading and return to it. Countless others would have had their reading appetites stimulated and eagerly gone on to devour other books after finishing the Harry Potter series. I think J.K. Rowling should go down in history as one of the major positive influences on children's reading and imaginations in the late 20th and early 21st centuries.

Returning to my fiction collection for a moment, Robert Louis Stevenson's "The Strange Case of Dr Jekyll and Mr Hyde" is another of the esteemed residents of my bookcase. It is one which I had been meaning to read for years but never quite got around to until recently. I was surprised to notice that a disproportionate number of my books were written by authors who were born, or now live in, Edinburgh. Edinburgh is a small city and seems to punch well above its weight in the literary field. Perhaps it's something in the haggis?

Robert Louis Stevenson also wrote a fascinating book about the city of his birth, titled: "Edinburgh - Picturesque Notes", which was first published in 1879. The book is a wonderful word portrait of the city and its surrounds, and the picture he paints reveals his strong emotional attachment to the subject. Despite the bond between them, Stevenson unflinchingly includes the negative character traits, as well as the positive. He thus deftly avoids creating a biased, one-dimensional view of this city and its citizens. The following, part of the story's opening passages, illustrates this beautifully.

*"The ancient and famous metropolis of the North sits overlooking a windy estuary from the slope and summit of three hills. No situation could be more commanding for the head city of a kingdom; none better chosen for noble prospects...*

*...But Edinburgh pays cruelly for her high seat in one of the vilest climates under heaven...*

*The weather is raw and boisterous in winter, shifty and ungenial in summer, and a downright meteorological purgatory in the spring. The delicate die early, and I, as a survivor, among bleak winds and plumping rain, have been sometimes tempted to envy them their fate. For all who love shelter and the blessings of the sun, who hate dark weather and perpetual tilting against squalls, there could scarcely be found a more unhomely and harassing place of residence. Many such aspire angrily after that Somewhere-else of the imagination, where all troubles are supposed to end. They lean over the great bridge which joins the New Town with the Old – that windiest spot, or high altar, in this northern temple of the winds – and watch the trains smoking out from under them and vanishing into the tunnel on a voyage to brighter skies... And yet the place establishes an interest in people's hearts; go where they will, they find no city of the same distinction; go where they will, they take a pride in their old home." (Stevenson, Edinburgh – Picturesque Notes)*

Stevenson describes a city steeped in history and recounts many a tale, of both fact and fiction, from the rich storehouse of Edinburghian lore. As a denizen of a relatively infant city - age wise - I am always fascinated by those metropolises which have accumulated many hundreds, sometimes thousands, of years of history within their boundaries. My city, Perth, had only been staking its claim on the Australian map for a scant fifty years at the time Stevenson's book was published.

Although obviously coming nowhere near the achievements of Edinburgh, during its development Perth saw many beautiful and grand buildings grace its streets. Unfortunately however, between 1960 and 1990, almost before the mortar was dry, the powers-that-be who decide such matters allowed acts of destruction that many of us feel the city will never recover from. It was a dark chapter in Perth's history when architectural genocide was committed on some of the most impressive 19th and early 20th century buildings, ravaging once-dignified street-scapes. Seizing their opportunity, skyscrapers, modern office blocks and shopping malls moved onto the newly-vacated land. Fortunately the people of Perth came to their senses in time to put a stop to this wanton destruction before every significant historical building was reduced to rubble, and legislation now prevents such a destructive splurge being repeated. The few survivors are dotted throughout the city centre, and hopefully their windows don't still tremble nervously every time a bulldozer goes past.

Because the majority of Perth's central business district is made up of relatively modern buildings, there is very little architectural connection to our past. The street-scapes of a hundred years ago no longer exist. Unless they accidentally came upon one of the few remaining colonial-era structures, newcomers to the city centre could be excused for assuming it had only been settled sometime in the twentieth century. To me, Perth feels as if it sits somewhat precariously on its foundations, its roots not reaching very deeply into the past to secure it firmly in its place in the world. In contrast, I imagine Edinburgh's rich cultural and historical heritage would engender a comforting sense of stability and permanence for its residents. Knowing that one's ancestors, or at least, fellow countrymen, have inhabited the same streets and buildings for hundreds of years would I presume, encourage a strong emotional connection to the city.

When visiting Scotland in 2005 I spent a few days in Glasgow, the birthplace and home of my great, great grandmother. While sitting on a park bench one afternoon, enjoying the sunshine and looking at the stately old buildings across the road, I had a sudden realisation. My grandmother could very well have gazed upon the same buildings, and perhaps even consciously admired them as I was now doing so many years and generations later. It was an emotional moment as I shared an experience with an ancestor who was long-dead before I was born. The beautiful old buildings had connected us for a brief instant across the seemingly non-bridgeable gap of time.

# CHAPTER FOUR

Although there are a number of books I haven't yet mentioned on the shelves of my bookcase, I am growing impatient to move on in my travels. I will return and refer to these neglected volumes later in the journey.

Heading east I come to a spindle-back chair, which is somewhat crotchety and infirm in its old age. It threatens to collapse in a pile of splintered wood if anyone attempts to rest on its time-worn seat. The chair, part of a dining set before its retirement, belonged to my maternal grandparents. It is a treasured and tangible link between my visits to their house and now.

Heirlooms and other objects that we keep as connections to people, places or events can be very effective repositories for our memories and emotions. Often we only need to glance at them for these treasures to be released. Sometimes however, over time the object, chameleon-like, begins to absorb the emotional tones of its new surroundings, becoming part of the current every-day events which flow around it. The original memories and emotions it holds become a little harder to access as the new environment overlays the old. Perhaps this is a good thing to some extent, particularly if we are surrounded by furniture and objects which hold strong associations with other places or times. Instead of being constantly assailed by sentiments from the past and being distracted from living in the present, we can choose when to make the effort required to access the memories lying dormant in our heirlooms and other possessions. For the rest of the time we can enjoy the objects for what they are now.

Perched on top of the spindle-backed chair is a hand-sewn cushion sporting a colourful Hawaiian design. The tropical themed rather plump cushion looks as if it has wandered onto the wrong chair, its natural environment more likely to be a sofa, but both of them appear happy with the unconventional arrangement.

When I decided on a tropical design for my sewing project, I didn't realise how difficult it would be to actually hunt down the material. Although there is seemingly a wide variety of designs readily available to us, whether it be in fabrics, furniture or houses, there are still themes that are "in" and "out" at any one time. Apparently I was totally out of step with the fashion gods, who had declared that Hawaiian was not the done thing at the moment. Luckily I managed to find a small remnant community of fabrics, the last survivors of the previous Hawaiian fashion trend of a few years ago. The gods will probably once again, at some point, decree that all things Hawaiian are the last word in good taste. The tropical motif will then be spilling off shelves and overflowing from shop doorways.

I am always bemused that something will be considered "attractive", "desirable" or the ultimate in "good taste" while it is in fashion, but the second it is superseded by the next "new thing", it is considered an embarrassment to own. The object has not changed one iota. What has changed is simply the attitude of those who get their opinions pre-packaged from the faceless style gurus, who hand down their decrees as if they were the word of God. It seems that most of us like to consider ourselves as having our own individual style, tastes, and ideas. However, at the same time we are often contradicting our own perceptions by carefully remaining within the boundaries which have been arbitrarily determined by others. We want to feel and be seen to be, part of the larger group, conforming to accepted norms of behaviour.

It is easy if the desired object can be found, as my Hawaiian fabric eventually was, to ignore fashion and follow our own tastes in the privately displayed areas of our lives. It does, however, take a lot more courage and self-confidence to blatantly sail in the face of convention in certain other aspects of our lives. One of these is in our choice of clothes. Today's clothing styles are very wide-ranging. From the latest trends, to certain eras of vintage, very few are options that would provoke a flurry of protest from disapproving on-lookers. There are still boundaries, however, to what is currently easily available and socially acceptable. Imagine a man who prefers the sartorial splendour of a distant by-gone age and chooses to go about his normal daily activities dressed in breeches, riding boots and an exquisitely ruffled shirt. Alternatively, perhaps he enjoys the simplicity and comfort of a Roman toga and sandals. Presumably he would have some difficulty in procuring such attire. Today's society has deemed such fashions to be beyond the pale and presume no-one would put himself to the blush by wearing such items outside of a fancy-dress party or a theatrical performance. It would be a man of considerable self-assurance who could step so far out of the accepted parameters of society and wear these types of clothes to work, a weekend barbeque, or the local shop. Although his choice of attire is just as valid – and probably more interesting – as those firmly swaddled in more current fashions, this man's appearance would almost certainly provoke ridicule and suspicion from many people. His detractors would feel threatened because he was behaving in a way that didn't fit into their narrow world-view of what was acceptable.

Even when some decide to break away from their society's dominant lifestyle, people usually find an alternative group to join, as the need to belong is such a strong human urge. Sub-cultures such as hippies, goths, and criminal gangs for example, may all have very different rules and customs from the wider society and from each other, but the individuals within them remain conformist to their own particular community.

The urge to conform to the wider group is not all bad of course, as it is the glue which holds society together, working towards common goals and mutual benefits. If we were all completely emotionally self-sufficient with no concern at all for obtaining the approval of others, there would be virtual anarchy. It is only when the need to follow the group without question, and resisting innovation or individual differences, is an automatic reflex, that this primal human instinct becomes destructive and limiting. The damage is avoided when people recognise that there are times when conforming is necessary for the well-being or survival of the group, and others when the choice should be left entirely with the individual, as the matter does not legitimately affect anyone else.

Before I resume my travels and arrive at my desk, here is De Maistre's account of his arrival at his writing bureau:

*"Leaving to the right the portraits of Raphael and his mistress, the Chevalier d'Assas and the Shepherdess of the Alps, and taking the left, the side on which the window is situated, my bureau comes into view. It is the first and the most prominent object the traveller's eyes light upon, taking the route I have indicated.*

*It is surmounted by a few shelves that serve as a book-case, and the whole is terminated by a bust which completes the* pyramid, and contributes more than any other object to the adornment of this region.

...In the opposite drawer lies a confused heap of materials for a touching history of the prisoner of Pignerol which, my dear friends, you will ere long read. Between these two drawers is a recess into which I throw whatever letters I receive. All that have reached me during the last ten years are there. The oldest of them are arranged according to date in several packets; the new ones lie pell-mell. Besides these, I have several dating from my early boyhood.

How great a pleasure it is to behold again through the medium of these letters the interesting scenes of our early years, to be once again transported into those happy days that we shall see no more!

...When I put my hand into this recess, I seldom leave the spot for the whole day. In like manner, a traveller will pass rapidly through whole provinces of Italy, making a few hurried and trivial observations on the way, and upon reaching Rome will take up his abode there for months.

This is the richest vein in the mine I am exploring. How changed I find my ideas and sentiments, and how altered do my friends appear when I examine them as they were in days gone by, and as they are now! In these mirrors of the past I see them in mortal agitation about plans which no longer disturb them.

Here I find an event announced which we evidently looked upon as a great misfortune; but the end of the letter is wanting, and the circumstance is so entirely forgotten that I cannot now make out what the matter was which so concerned us. We were possessed by a thousand prejudices. We knew nothing of the world, and of men. But then, how warm was our intercourse! How intimate our friendship! How unbounded our confidence!

*In our ignorance there was bliss. But now, - ah! All is now changed. We have been compelled, as others, to read the human heart; and truth, falling like a bomb into the midst of us, has forever destroyed the enchanted palace of illusion."*

*(De Maistre, A Journey Round My Room, p. 99 - 103)*

Having left my chair behind I now arrive at my desk, which has become the command post for the duration of my journey. I write my travel notes here, surrounded by an ever-increasing collection of reference books, scribbled notes, pens and general debris that appears, seemingly, from nowhere. I always use pens and lined pads rather than the computer when writing my early drafts. It's only when the piece is ready for its final tweaking that I take advantage of technology and transfer it into my lap-top. Even though my handwriting is barely legible at times as I try to get my thoughts recorded before they escape without trace, I find that I can think more clearly using this method. Perhaps it is because I grew up writing by hand, so my brain connects the act of creative thinking to holding a pen and making squiggles on a piece of paper. That said though, many of my contemporaries find that their creative juices flow more freely into the computer than onto the page.

Usually within minutes of beginning, my page is covered with sentences scratched out with ink, new ideas squeezed between lines, and arrows in every direction showing where extra information is to be inserted. The page soon looks like a word-soaked battleground with dead and dying sentences everywhere. I know it would be much easier to edit my work and leave it with a shred of dignity by using the computer, but this wouldn't help much if I couldn't think of anything to write.

Some educational authorities are concerned that the current generation of school children may effectively be losing the ability to write by hand because they do so much of their work on the computer. These educators are calling for more time to be spent on teaching and practising basic handwriting skills. Technologies such as computers have their place, but that place shouldn't be Everywhere. It is only very recently, historically speaking, that so many societies have managed to achieve high rates of literacy for their people. It would be a major step backwards if future generations only knew how to write using a piece of machinery. What happens if all of our technology is rendered useless in the future, through some as-yet-unimagined event? We wouldn't just be set back to pre-computer times, but effectively to the pre-literacy period if everyone's ability to write was trapped inside suddenly useless bits of metal and plastic.

Everyone has their own preferences on writing materials, perhaps a few still like to use a freshly plucked goose feather as a quill, which is their prerogative if that's what they choose. (Although the goose may not agree.) The whole point is that we have a choice and we owe it to future generations to ensure that they also have one.

Standing guard duty on top of some otherwise footloose papers is a resin paperweight. Implanted within it are heads of wheat, which are a minute portion of the final crop harvested on our farm before it was sold. These pieces of grain are the only physical part of the farm that I now have.

My childhood was spent on our wheat farm on the outer fringes of the eastern wheat belt of Western Australia. In many ways it was an idyllic environment for my two siblings and me to do our growing up in, having virtually unrestricted access to a 1,200 hectare (3,000 acre) playground. My deep appreciation for, and bond with nature is presumably a result of having been immersed in it during these formative years. Our property was situated in a low rainfall area, with hot dry summers and jaw numbingly cold winters. The trees were predominately spindly-trunked mallees and other eucalypts, with an under-storey of dusky green, thin leafed shrubs. The plants took their colours from a more muted palette than the one used by their counterparts in the Perth area, but my family and I loved the harsh semi-arid beauty of the landscape.

The natural environment was an intrinsic part of my childhood and it plays a leading role in many of my fondest memories from this time. One of these is of Mum, my brother, sister and I making our annual trek to an area covered in granite rocks. The crevices filled with water in winter and the resulting rock pools would soon teem with tadpoles. Some members of these amphibious communities, presumably to their considerable surprise, would suddenly find themselves being gently scooped up and deposited into water-filled jars. We would keep them until they were almost frogs, before repatriating them back to their original homes.

The rocky outcrops were surrounded by bush and another of our yearly rituals was to search the area for donkey and spider orchids. These would usually be hiding demurely in the undergrowth, making the search and discovery into something of a treasure hunt. Donkey and spider orchids are very delicate, quite small flowers and just as beautiful but not nearly as ostentatious as their more flamboyant tropical cousins. As far as I am aware, they are never seen inside the confines of florist shops. Mum taught us how to pick our floral treasures once we had found them. We would be very careful to break them cleanly off at the stem without disturbing their roots so as to ensure their return the following year.

The bush provided an ever-changing bounty for the senses, depending on the season. In spring the ground would be carpeted with pink everlasting flowers, their papery petals still living up to their name long after being re-housed into vases. The wide variety of shrubs would celebrate the balmy spring days by adorning themselves in colourful displays of tiny, fragile flowers. During the heat of summer the air would be thickened with eucalyptus oils, creating the distinctive scent of perspiring gum trees. Even now, the slightest whiff of eucalypt evokes nostalgic memories of the mallee country for me. The bush was also home to a multitude of different creatures, including kangaroos, emus, goannas and echidnas, so at times it was filled with noises and movement as they went about their business.

The bush also had it secrets, which it would share with those lucky enough to stumble across them. When I began attending the local school in 1967 it consisted of one small asbestos classroom and two tiny corrugated-iron sheds which housed the toilets. The grounds were surrounded by the natural bush from which they had been carved. The school population numbered approximately ten students of various ages and a young male teacher. Our teacher would occasionally lead the class on a nature walk through the bush, following vaguely defined trails or forging our own. On one of these excursions we discovered the remnants of an old cottage which was quietly basking in the dappled sunshine of a small clearing. It's partly crumbled walls and missing roof told us that it had been left to enjoy its own company for many years. The collective instinct of each child there was to immediately explore this exciting discovery, but to our disappointment we were forbidden to do so. The crumbling mud-brick walls could not be relied upon to accept the intrusion of clambering children gracefully. Over the years, as I sat in my classroom a short walk away, I sometimes wondered about the lives of those earlier settlers and what might have happened to them. I loved knowing the ruin was out there, as it was a tangible relic from the past. Although nature was re-claiming it, it had decided to do so slowly and patiently, and for that, I was glad.

Although growing up in the country meant missing out on some of the activities and amenities city kids would have taken for granted, my siblings and I were not short of equally rewarding experiences. I learned to drive a car by the age of ten and revelled in the freedom of rattling along the dusty farm tracks in a battered old Austin A40. At other times we enjoyed riding around our property on an off-road motorbike.

Many areas, such as rainforests, snow-capped mountain vistas or palm fringed beaches have an instant appeal because of the dramatic and attractive statement they make. At first glance the landscape of my childhood may have appeared dry and semi-barren, particularly during the harsh summer days when survival could be a challenge for both plant and animal. Upon closer inspection however, its subtle beauty and richness became delightfully obvious.

Although we only lived approximately four hours drive by car from Perth, our rural community was markedly different to the city. It was something of a culture shock each time we visited the metropolis to see family and friends a few times a year. One special memory I have is of watching a cowboy movie on my grandparents' new television, the very first time I had ever seen one on a colour screen. I adored "Westerns", and the excitement of actually seeing coloured horses riding through spectacular coloured scenery had me virtually slack-jawed in wonderment. It was in stark contrast to our black and white television at home, with its reception so fuzzy the signal may well have been sent via Russia. Despite such technological excitements however, it was always fun to get home to the farm again.

I delighted in our farm and enjoyed attending the bush school, but a part of me was often in far-away lands or times, transported there through the countless books I read and the few television shows I saw. Tales set in historic English villages, surrounded by rolling green pastures dotted with sheep, were very attractive. Particularly when compared to the dust and dizzying heat of an Australian outback summer. Similarly, police dramas set in big American cities provided glimpses into exotic worlds far beyond my limited personal experience.

Our family sold the farm and moved to Perth when I was fifteen. Despite my love of the bush and its lifestyle, I always knew I would leave it someday as the role of farmer's wife later on was one I would never consider. I was happy to move to the city, excited about beginning a new chapter, with its promise of opportunities and adventures. Emotionally it wasn't a clean break from my childhood however, as the bush had become an intrinsic part of me. I knew I was psychologically unsuited to spending my adult life in the bush, but the city proved to be an uncomfortable fit for a long time. I have now lived in Perth for most of my adult life but there is still a part of my spirit that really only responds to the natural environment, wherever it may be. It's no wonder people re-locating from one country to another so often find the transition difficult. Even when the reasons for leaving a homeland are compelling, our original environments leave a lasting impression, whether good or bad.

Often what we miss from our earlier lives and feel we have left behind no longer exists. Migrants, whether from overseas or the neighbouring suburb, upon returning to recapture the experience of home after a long period away, are often shocked to find that Time has left its mark as it passed through. Although superficially things may appear to be the same, there are myriads of changes, both big and small, woven into what is still familiar. In my case, a subsequent owner of our farm removed the transportable asbestos house we had called home. Paddocks and vast swathes of bushland had also been altered radically. As with many rural regions the population of the area had dwindled over the years, so the local school had been closed down and some of its buildings removed. I will probably never return to the farm to visit it, as the reality we once knew no longer exists outside of my imagination and those of my family. I would prefer to keep that reality safe by not tampering with the recollections of what was. There's no way we can really recapture the parts of our past that we miss; as life as well as we ourselves, has inexorably moved on.

Also sitting on my desk is a model plane, mounted on a stand and positioned in a permanent pose of simulated flight. Although it's official role is purely decorative it is often seconded to be a back-up paperweight and deployed to various unruly paper situations.

I have always been fascinated by anything that manages to escape the bonds of gravity. It seems appropriate that my earliest memory, at the age of two, is of being strapped into the seat of a helicopter by my Dad and then waving excitedly to Mum as the pilot lifted us heavenwards. Mum was heavily pregnant with my soon-to-be baby sister and had decided to remain securely earthbound.

During my childhood one of our neighbours' sons, who was some years older than me, would regularly pass his comics, books and magazines onto us once he had read them. These ranged from Donald Duck comics to cowboy novels, war comics, and more. Being a voracious reader I enthusiastically devoured them all, including the comics which were based on World War 2. I soon knew how many crew members were needed for a Lancaster bomber, and what role the Spitfires played. I found myself in awe of both the fear and courage that the pilots must have felt while engaging in a "dogfight" over enemy territory. This early reading material sparked my interest in the military, particularly the air force. A family outing to an open day at the RAAF Pearce air force base when I was fifteen fuelled it even further. Probably the most magical moment for me, in a day filled with memorable impressions, was the low-level fly-past of an F1-11 fighter jet. The crowd had been warned to cover their ears as it approached, as it would be breaking the sound barrier. As the sonic boom washed over us I thought that it was one of the most impressive sounds I had ever heard. By the time we were back in the car and driving home later that afternoon I knew where my destiny lay. I would join the air force.

When I turned seventeen, the minimum entry age, I was employed as a clerical assistant in a state government department, having left school just over a year earlier. My desire to join the air force was still there, but dormant at that point. I was very introverted and didn't have the confidence to apply, so I put it on hold for sometime in the future. This fear induced inertia was banished mere weeks later however, when a friend from high school suddenly announced that she was going to apply. Her excitement was so contagious it allayed my fears and I too was soon reporting to the recruitment centre for aptitude, psychological and medical testing.

At the end of the day's tests I was told that I had passed them all with good marks. All except one. Unfortunately it was not a test I could try again later, as it was my very poor eyesight which had been the deal-breaker. Although the air force didn't require its members to have perfect vision, it did have a bottom line and I was very much below it. With the aid of industrial-strength lenses my eyesight is, I assume, on a par with the average. Without my glasses I can't even safely cross the road on my own, as objects only a couple of metres away are a blur. Naturally I was bitterly disappointed and upset at this news. A career doorway I had naively assumed would probably be open for me whenever I was ready to step through had just slammed shut with a resounding thud. Fortunately my friend passed and within weeks she was heading off to an air force base in the eastern states. I was very pleased for her, but it was painful knowing I would never be making the same journey.

Although it took some time to get over the intense disappointment, once I had come to terms with it I was happy that I had applied, despite not being accepted. I had made a grab for my dream, and as I get older I am even more grateful to my seventeen year old self that I did. If I hadn't, I'm quite sure that the intervening decades would have been filled with "If only I had applied", and "Why didn't I?" self-recriminations. I would have lived under the delusion that I had passed up an exciting opportunity, when in reality it had never been there in the first place. I have also retained my fascination with military jets, with their impressive speed and manoeuvrability, and get a rush whenever I see one fly overhead. Over time perhaps this admiration would have transformed into dislike if my psyche had been haunted by unexplored opportunities regarding the air force. The sleek airborne marvels of technology may have become an unwelcome reminder of my own youthful cowardice.

When I was in England in 2005 I had what I felt was a slightly surreal experience involving a British fighter jet. I was standing near a section of Hadrian's Wall, which runs from east to west across northern England. The wall dates back to AD122 when the first stones were laid during the rule of Emperor Hadrian. Although there are various theories as to its purpose, one of the popular ones is that it was to protect Roman Britain from being invaded by the Scots. Although no longer maintaining the majestic height it once enjoyed, having succumbed to the ravages of Time and human plundering of its stones, the wall is still an impressive example of ancient endeavour. As I stood gazing at it and marvelling at its age, I heard the roar of a fighter jet overhead. Looking up, Past and Present seemed to compress into a single moment. Examples of AD122 defence technology and that of almost 2000 years later were juxtaposed into a single scene.

A slide-out keyboard shelf under my desk-top holds my medical records, many of which, including x-rays and a variety of other scans, are too large to fit into a conventional drawer. I will only spend a few moments here, as reminders of past procedures and tests are rarely a good place to linger. Before I move on, a brief comment about the current medical condition which is responsible for ensuring that I maintain a close relationship with my house, will be enough.

A heart attack in January 2008, at the age of forty-six, triggered off a moderate bout of chronic fatigue syndrome.

My health slowly improved, and a year later the chronic fatigue had subsided to a manageable level. In late 2009 a handful of other medical hiccups caused the fatigue to flare up again, this time severely, which resulted in my having a physical meltdown. This situation is hopefully only temporary, but there's no knowing how long it will last.

The drawers either side of my desk are of even less interest than the medical records, holding assorted stationery and household files, so it is time to explore new territory. On the wall behind the desk is a large framed black and white picture of New York's Grand Central Station. The photo was taken circa. 1930 and shows beams of light streaming through the large windows and into the crowded hall below. The shafts of light almost appear to be made of solidified sunshine, they are so strongly defined. Not surprisingly, due to this somewhat surreal visual effect the photo has become a classic.

Because it depicts a scene which is over eighty years old, the people who were simply extras in the bigger picture at the time are now also an interesting aspect of it. Almost all of the people are wearing hats, and not a single baseball cap amongst them, which is a sure indicator of a by-gone age. The men are, almost without exception, dressed in an identical style of overcoat, unlike our modern eclectic tastes and options. It is fascinating to imagine the world these commuters would have re-entered upon stepping out of the station, compared to that of today's traveller. As I look at the photo, I imagine Grand Central Station as a giant Time Portal. In many ways it remains essentially the same as it was in 1930, while over the decades succeeding generations have passed through it into a constantly changing outside world.

Photos are our glimpses back into the past, but it is such a necessarily restricted view that it is akin to peering through a pinhole in the fabric of time. Every time we take a photo we are using the camera's aperture to create our pinhole. We are determining which moment and scene will be captured and potentially preserved indefinitely while others only centimetres or seconds away are lost forever.

The image on my wall is black and white, as were the vast majority of photos taken before the mid 1930's. In 1935 commercially available, simple to use colour film was introduced. I find that some photos actually benefit from being purely black and white. I think nature usually demands the full colour palette be plundered when she is having her portrait done, but not all subjects are so choosy. Sometimes urban environments such as buildings and street scenes are shown to their best advantage in monochrome rather than colour. Perhaps this is because their components are more obvious when the observer isn't distracted by a multitude of colours. The eye is then more drawn to the lines and structures themselves. Similarly, portraits of people can at times be more dramatic when their features are reduced to black and white and the various shades of these. Having said all that, colour has added a wonderfully rich dimension to our photos, in all categories. It would be alarming if we still had a world where "you can have a photo in any colour you like, as long as it's black and white".

# CHAPTER FIVE

My next stop is the floor-to-ceiling window which looks out onto a garden, where the leafy occupants are visibly wilting. It is a ferociously hot summer day of 41 degrees Celsius when I reach the window, and I am very glad of the split-system air-conditioner high on the wall, which is working hard to ensure my travelling comfort.

On weekends, depending on the season, the sounds of people cheering on their football teams, or clapping when a good hit is made in cricket, float through the window from the large park across the road. The tantalising aroma of sausage-sizzles also wafts over on the breeze. Depending on my mood, these tokens of normal everyday life are at times almost comforting. They are a sign that our society is basically safe and functions well, with people free to enjoy themselves as they choose. At other times these same sounds and smells accentuate the fact that I'm very much on the fringes of life at the moment, a spectator rather than participant. These negative interpretations don't happen very often, as usually the crowd noise is merely a neutral backdrop to the day.

Part of the park contains a stand of large eucalyptus trees which attract a variety of birds, including pink and grey galahs. These galahs always look cheeky, as if they're gleefully planning some practical joke or have just successfully carried one out. This impression is in direct contrast to the personality of another type of bird that occasionally enlivens my garden. The willy-wagtail is tiny, rotund, black and white with a long tail and a very bad attitude. It was a long time before I realised they actually had a birdsong in their vocal repertoire because they are usually swearing at something or other. One I saw started chattering in annoyance every time it began to rain, only stopping when each brief shower passed. These cute feather-balls are fearless as well as grumpy. They are often to be seen chasing crows, possibly for the sheer thrill of it.

Crows also like to congregate in the park's eucalypts, cawing loudly to each other. They are probably complaining about the irksome willy-wagtails. Even though I've heard them countless times over the years, their cawing often brings one memory to mind – walking across a paddock with my grandfather and dad, looking at some new lambs and hearing the crows in the trees. This is the only memory the crows' call brings back spontaneously, perhaps because it is one of the few memories I have of Granddad before he became ill and virtually bed-ridden. It's interesting how the mind responds to certain stimuli, often ignoring the multitude of more recent or current memories associated with it, and consistently leaping onto one which may be decades old. It is unfortunate that this eccentricity is not always benign, as it can be distressing if the activated memories are painful.

Living near a busy road, the footpaths outside my house see a lot of human and canine traffic. This is sometimes mildly diverting when a noteworthy example of either species wanders past. Regretfully I've never seen anything more exotic than dogs being walked, unlike some fortunate and probably bemused Parisians, who may have had an interesting anecdote to recount to their friends. Sometime during the 19th century a French poet, Gerard de Nerval, allegedly took his pet lobster for walks in the gardens of the Palais – Royal, on the end of a long blue ribbon. I say 'allegedly' because literary scholars and marine biologists disagree about the veracity of this legend. Whether true or not, because people like a good eccentricity tale, the story has managed to ignore the sceptics and remains firmly embedded in folklore.

Between my study and the street is my garden, a welcome buffer-zone separating my private sanctuary and the public arena. Outside the window a gardenia which had panicked about being transplanted from another part of the garden, and wildly shed its leaves in agitation, has recovered from the attack of nerves. It is now happily re-clothing itself in a profusion of bright green foliage. My garden is an invaluable emotional re-charger for me, even a few minutes spent wandering aimlessly around the backyard can noticeably improve my sense of well-being.

Many believe nature has its own energy and I agree, how else could it be so calming, particularly when we venture into natural forests or bushland, or onto rivers, lakes or oceans? Dad planted an acorn in his backyard approximately eighteen years ago and it is now a good-sized oak tree with a large canopy of bright-green leaves. I was surprised to discover, while standing under this canopy one day, that there was a subtle but noticeable change in how I felt. It was as if the tree was emanating a calm energy. Wondering if I was imagining it, I repeatedly stepped in and out of the area covered by the tree's branches and felt a mild but perceptible difference each time.

In stark contrast to the natural world I find that highly artificial surroundings, such as shopping malls, suck the energy out of me. Even if I have gone to the mall quite happily, intent on some purchasing conquest or other, it only takes half an hour or so before I'm questioning my will to live. The cacophony of noise from piped music blaring out of various shops and the chatter of the crowds is a contributing factor to the resulting claustrophobia. Another is having to dodge and weave to avoid bumping into those who dart out of shop doorways, seemingly with their eyes shut, or others who stop suddenly in mid-step as some gew-gaw in a window catches their eye. Perhaps the major reason that soon sends me searching for an exit is that the natural environment is rarely welcome inside a large shopping mall. With artificially bright lighting, plastic plants, the previously mentioned excessive noise levels and the entire sprawling megaplex constructed of concrete, it is an assault on the senses.

As I write this I stop and gaze out of the window for a few moments. The sky is cloudless and a deceptively mild breeze is ruffling the leaves on the frangipani tree. Although the languid wind appears innocuous, it is coming from the east and bringing the desert heat with it. The air-conditioner is earning its keep this season. Perth is preparing itself for what is expected to be a record-breaking week or more of temperatures above 35 degrees C. Incredible to think that on the other side of the country in Northern New South Wales, large areas have been evacuated due to severe flooding.

A few vehicles go past, some of them proudly flying small Australian flags which are attached to their roofs and flapping in the slip-stream. Today is Australia Day and a public holiday. Unlike many cities which have spectacular fireworks displays on New Year's Eve, Perth saves it for today, setting them off from barges on the Swan River in the centre of the city, and from the rooftops of the tallest buildings. These fireworks are always very impressive and draw large crowds. Getting home afterwards can be difficult as thousands of people valiantly attempt to all leave the city at once. It's no wonder officials everywhere dread the prospect of ever having to evacuate a whole city, when it takes so long to move just a small proportion of the population out of an area. Add panic and confusion to the mix and it would truly be the stuff of nightmares.

# CHAPTER SIX

Breaking camp once again, I travel away from the window and arrive at my roll-top desk which sits against the adjoining wall. The desk was a twenty-first birthday present from Mum and Dad and has travelled with me through my adulthood, settling comfortably into a succession of different homes along the way.

On top of my desk sit stuffed toys of Sesame Street's Ernie and Bert. Bert's expression suggests he is somewhat baffled about how and why he is there, while Ernie as usual appears quite happy with his circumstances. As a child I had enjoyed watching Ernie's antics on Sesame Street, so when I came across him in an ABC shop one day I spontaneously bought him, thinking he would add a light-hearted touch to my study. The following Christmas my son, deciding that Ernie needed his Bert, bought him for me as a gift.

As I was writing this I felt slightly embarrassed at admitting to buying a stuffed Sesame Street toy for myself. After thinking about it for a moment however, I realised I had nothing to feel embarrassed about. People the world over collect all manner of objects for all sorts of reasons. Whether it be soft toys, signed sporting memorabilia, Smurf figurines or just about anything imaginable, it is all a way of remembering or owning something that is important or nostalgic to us.

The desire to capture the atmosphere and magic of television shows, movies, books, sporting events and the like, is a very strong one for many people, children and adults alike. Every children's movie that becomes a box-office hit has corresponding merchandise such as toys, lunch-boxes and anything else that can be licensed, to allow the audience to feel they "own" a piece of it. Adults pay, on occasion, huge prices for movie, sports and music memorabilia such as dresses worn by legendary actresses, or guitars previously owned by music icons. We hope that by owning something representing an event or a story, we will be able to bring a trace of that world into our own. To varying degrees, sometimes it actually does.

My study is very much a mixture of objects and themes, but it is full of what is important to me and I find it a relaxing and pleasant environment to be in. That is a benefit of having "a room of one's own", it doesn't matter if the décor would cause an interior designer to shriek in despair. In our own spaces we have the freedom to be who we are.

My laptop computer sits on my desk, an indispensable companion throughout my current journey, readily providing me with information on a multitude of subjects along the way. Looking at it, I marvel at its deceptively innocuous appearance, considering that it is a portal into the world. Although my son's generation take it for granted, having never known life to be any other way, the powers of the internet still retain a whiff of magic for me. It's as if everyone of my generation and older grew up with a set of well-recognised laws of physics and then suddenly a new one was added, which became known as the internet.

I wonder what De Maistre would have made of the internet, and the fact that he is featured on it? If, as one school of thought speculates, reincarnation exists, perhaps he has not only seen it but regularly uses the internet in his current incarnation. What a pity that even if this was the case, he wouldn't remember his life as De Maistre. That is the situation for all of us of course, if there is any such thing as reincarnation none of us have any idea who we may have been. Apart that is, from those people who go to psychics and then claim to know their previous identities. It is unbelievable – literally – how many have been Cleopatra or other exotic famous figures. I've not heard of many who discover they were peasants or serving wenches.

If we are on return visits to the mortal realm, imagine all of the bizarre situations that could occur without us being aware of them. For example, Joe Bloggs may be reading a book written by an author who had died before he was born, and in a strange twist of fate both the reader and the writer are Joe Bloggs. Or perhaps a sick baby is saved by a medical breakthrough she herself had discovered in her previous life.

I quite like the idea of multiple lives, but only if we have some say in who we come back as. Perhaps it's a matter of nominating for up-coming vacancies? If so, I imagine the spots where the applicants will be devastatingly intelligent, attractive and born into mega-wealthy families would fill quickly. In contrast, vacancies to be born into a family of seriously in-bred criminals may need conscripts to fill. Whether De Maistre is somewhere at this moment, perhaps sipping a latte in a New York cafe, or he's not, I find the idea of re-incarnation an intriguing one.

The laptop reminds me of a story I recently read. Written by Charles Dickens, and titled "Some Account of an Extraordinary Traveller" it is a light-hearted report about Mr Booley, a sixty-five year old Englishman, and his incredible world travels. The story was originally published in the weekly periodical, Household Words, in April 1850. There are some details within the narrative which don't appear to quite fit, such as the following:

*"Mr Booley's powers of endurance are wonderful. All climates are alike to him. Nothing exhausts him; no alterations of heat and cold appear to have the least effect upon his hardy frame. His capacity of travelling, day and night, for thousands of miles, has never been approached by any traveller of whom we have any knowledge through the help of books........Though remarkable for personal cleanliness, he has carried no luggage; and his diet has been of the simplest kind. He has often found a biscuit, or a bun, sufficient for his support over a vast tract of country." (Dickens)*

The story is sprinkled with clues that "something is afoot" as Dickens describes the various expeditions Mr Booley embarks on, such as to New Orleans where he explores the Mississippi and Missouri rivers by steamboat. After completing a multitude of excursions, Mr Booley suspends his travels long enough to catch up with friends at his private London club, the Social Oysters. Comfortably ensconced in an armchair this traveller extraordinaire tells his attentive audience:

*"It is very gratifying to me", said he, "to have seen so much at my time of life, and to have acquired a knowledge of the countries I have visited, which I could not have derived from books alone. When I was a boy, such travelling would have been impossible, as the gigantic-moving-panorama or diorama mode of conveyance, which I have principally adopted (all my modes of conveyance have been pictorial), had then not been attempted. It is a delightful characteristic of these times, that new and cheap means are continually being devised for conveying the results of actual experience to those who are unable to obtain such experiences for themselves: and to bring them within the reach of the people – emphatically of the people; for it is they at large who are addressed in these endeavours, and not exclusive*

*audiences. Hence", said Mr Booley, "even if I see a run on an idea, like the panorama one, it awakens no ill-humour within me, but gives me pleasant thoughts. Some of the best results of actual travel are suggested by such means to those whose lot it is to stay at home. New worlds open out to them, beyond their little worlds, and widen their range of reflection, information, sympathy, and interest. The more man knows of man, the better for the common brotherhood among us all." (Dickens, Some Account of an Extraordinary Traveller)*

Dickens made it obvious that there was a twist in the tale, but it was not until the end that the reader discovered exactly what form it took. The panoramas, or dioramas, that Mr Booley used for his travels consisted of large scenes painted on both sides of a canvas, and displayed in a theatre. Through clever lighting effects the audience would see the scene slowly change, sometimes from day to night, or to something completely different. The diorama was first exhibited in London in 1823 and was a huge success. As Dickens said, it gave people the opportunity to catch glimpses of the wider world. Photography had yet to be invented, and only the wealthy had the means to travel abroad.

I particularly enjoyed Dickens' account of Mr Booley's adventures because he used a substitute for the real travel experience – the Diorama. Before reading Dickens' story, I had thought about how effective the internet is for embarking on virtual travel adventures. Although this method is obviously not ideal, it is a window into the wider world for those who cannot experience it in the first person, just as the Diorama was for the people in Dickensian times. It sits somewhere between the written travelogue, which requires a considerable use of imagination by the reader, and reality, where it is fully packaged and presented. After reading Dickens' story I thought it could be fun to try my hand at using the internet to write a realistic travel article, on a place I had never actually been to. I imagined that it would be a considerable challenge to make it accurate enough to convince those who are actually familiar with the chosen destination, and to give it an authentic first person flavour. Up to now, the idea has remained just that, an idea, but Now seems a good time to take a side-trip before I continue exploring my desk.

Turning my computer on, I complete the necessary preparations for my excursion, which consist solely of choosing a destination. I have the advantage over Mr Booley because there is no need for me to even leave the house to begin my "adventure". After some indecision, I finally decide to 'travel' to Central Park in New York City. The following is an account of my visits to the park.

## PARKING IN NEW YORK

As the last of the children were lifted or had scrambled onto their horses, big grins of happy anticipation were securely fixed to most of the young faces. A few, perhaps complete novices, weren't sure whether fear or excitement was their dominant emotion. One of the youngest suddenly decided which feeling to go with, and tearfully demanded to be helped off his colourfully attired steed. A new rider was quickly recruited, and the whole group began to move as one, accompanied by the classic melody of calliope music.

As I stood and watched the carousel do its rounds I was momentarily transported away from the idyllic spring day in Central Park, New York City. I was briefly on a much smaller but equally magical carousel version from my own childhood, the music, colour and movement imprinted firmly on my memory. With 57 horses, the Central Park Carousel is one of the largest in the United States, and was crafted in 1908 in the American Folk Art style. It is one of the Park's favourite attractions, with its horses enticing almost 250,000 riders onto their backs each year. It's comforting to know that some childhood entertainments are relatively timeless.

I came across the Carousel on the first of a number of forays into the Park, during my visit to New York City. It is sheer luck that this beautiful carousel is now kept busy creating life-long memories for many of its young riders. Discovered abandoned on Coney Island, it was rescued and re-housed in its current position. Each of the horses either has been, or is in the process of, being restored to their former colourful glory. Central Park itself has endured mixed fortunes – at various times throughout its history it has fallen into neglect and/or disrepute.

Today the Park is managed by the Central Park Conservancy, which was founded in 1980 in response to the dramatic decline of the area in the 1970's. Since its formation the Conservancy has succeeded in transforming the Park into the show-piece it is today.

Central Park was first opened in 1857. The city commissioner sponsored a public competition, won by Frederick Law Olmsted and Calvert Vaux in 1858, to create a design which would transform it from the treeless, rocky and swampy area it then was. One of the surprising aspects of the Park, for me, was its size. Aerial views don't give a true picture of just how big its 843 acres feel, when one is actually inside what has often been called "the lungs of the city". The area is made up of a wide range of landscapes. These include the 55 acre Great Lawn in the centre, the Reservoir which covers 106 acres, and the Conservatory Garden – a formal area planted in a variety of styles, including Italian. There are also a number of woodland areas, with paths and hiking trails winding through them. These are only a few examples, with too many to list in full without exhausting the reader's patience.

The Park has something for everyone, with a wide range of activities and attractions on offer. Children are well catered for. Apart from giving them the opportunity to explore and enjoy the natural environment, there are two zoos, one of which is specifically designed for children, with a variety of interactive activities. There are 21 playgrounds, each with its own individual characteristics. Statues are positioned at various spots throughout the Park. While most of them are strictly for visual appreciation, others are designed especially for children to climb on. On one of my walks I came across a bronze likeness of Alice in Wonderland sitting on a toadstool. The Mad Hatter and White Rabbit were keeping her company, as were three or four children, one of whom was energetically testing whether the animal's ears were detachable or not. Harlem Meer, an artificial lake, has a catch-and-release fishing program which is very popular with families. Rods and bait are supplied and advice given on how to avoid harming the fish or resident wildlife. The Recreation Centre runs regular sports clinics and tournaments for people of all ages.

I discovered that an ideal place to people watch is from a bench somewhere along the Mall. Located in the middle of the Park, this 40- foot- wide, paved pedestrian path runs from 66th to 72nd streets. Both sides are lined by large American elm trees, their canopies reaching towards each other to form a picturesque, leafy arch. The southern end is named the Literary Walk, due to the statues depicting famous writers which are placed at intervals along it. These impressive figures are set just off the path behind the low rail fencing, and include Shakespeare and Robert Burns. Somewhat incongruously in this literary line-up, Christopher Columbus is also there. Perhaps it is because he was responsible for a pivotal chapter being written in the American history books? Old-style black lamp-posts also line the path and with all of the elements combined, there is a lovely almost-old-fashioned air to the Mall.

Central Park is a very popular location for film and television crews. Since the very early years of cinema, hundreds of movies have included scenes shot within its boundaries. It has also been part of countless other television series episodes. For example, various fictional police and forensic T.V. shows have placed their murder victims in some secluded spot or another. Luckily these gruesome scenes are purely works of fiction, however there were periods in the Park's history where it wasn't the best place to be, as far as personal safety was concerned. Today Central Park is a very safe place and according to statistics, in the real world there were no murders or rapes within its boundaries in 2011 and none so far in 2012. There is also a low rate of minor crime. The Park is patrolled by the New York City Parks Enforcement Patrol and the New York Police Department. I was hoping to come across a film crew, especially one from a show I am familiar with, working on a new episode, but no such luck.

The most memorable of my Central Park experiences would have to be the couple of hours I spent in the Ramble. This 38-acre woodland is an impressive example of what can be achieved when Man and Nature combine forces. Walking through this area, it is hard to believe that every tree and bush in it has been especially planted to create an environment that appears to have evolved naturally. I was surprised to discover that even the stream, with its water rippling over the rocks, is artificial. Even structures which have the unmistakable fingerprint of human creativity stamped onto them blend in seamlessly with their surroundings. While walking along a footpath through a crowded thicket of trees and shrubbery, I came to a picturesque arch positioned in a crevice which divides two rocky outcrops. The arch was mainly built from rocks found in the Park, and as a result it was easy to imagine that it had simply grown into the space.

The Ramble is a bird-watchers' nirvana, particularly around the vicinity of the Azalea Pond. The pond gets its name from the azalea bushes that adorn its southern bank, which were ablaze with a profusion of pink blooms, as spring was at Nature's controls for the moment. It was an idyllic spot to sit and simply Be for a while, on one of the benches overlooking the water. Watching the wide variety of birds flitting overhead from branch to branch, and squirrels sprinting up trees, I had to remind myself that I was still in the middle of one of the planet's most densely built-up cities.

The Manhattan skyline can be seen from many areas of Central Park. This visual reminder of the stark contrast between the Park and its surroundings enhances the impression of a calm oasis within a vibrant and busy cityscape. It appears to be a symbiotic relationship, with the Park allowing a "time-out" from the fast-paced city, and re-energising its visitors for their return to that environment. The city's streets in their turn welcome their citizens back, providing them with the entertainment and faster, more dynamic pace that is outside the Park's mission statement.

I only managed to sample a small proportion of the Park's many attractions and due to space issues, have included even less in this article. For example I have not even touched on the modes of transport available such as pedi-cabs, or the extensive range of guided tours. I would imagine that a resident of New York could visit it regularly for a life-time and not grow tired of Central Park, as what it has to offer is so diverse and plentiful.

...

I have now returned from my virtual side-trip to Central Park and as I thought, there was a wealth of information, both written and visual, about it on the internet. My main challenge in attempting to write about it in the above piece was choosing what to include and what to leave out. The article may be riddled with errors, making it an obvious work of fiction to anyone who knows the Park, but I'm hoping this is not the case. I do feel as if I have visited Central Park on a strange twilight level, somewhere between reality and complete imagination. This is probably due to having spent many hours immersed in the various relevant websites, deliberately trying to picture myself there. I now have a collection of images in my memory, obtained from photos of scenes in the Park. If I didn't know better than to believe it, these images, combined with my imagination, could almost be confused with real experiences as far as my memory is concerned. Although obviously far inferior to the real thing, the internet is definitely a travel option of sorts for those who can't physically experience exotic locations, for whatever reason. I think Dickens' Mr Booley would have thoroughly enjoyed this mode of travel. He would need to have been warned however, getting a virtual taste stimulates the appetite for the real deal.

A week or two after returning from my "trip" I was watching a fictional police procedural on television when the action moved to a part of Central Park. It was an area I had "visited" and as I watched the scene unfold I had a powerful sensation that I was seeing a place I was personally familiar with, which was rather fun.

My desk's various cubby-holes display an assortment of souvenirs from my own and family members' various trips to Britain. One of these is a tiny and very cute amber owl made in Suffolk, England and given to me by my sister. Before beginning its new life as a pretend owl this honey-coloured carving was resin from a tree that may have lived millions of years ago. Although this particular piece doesn't, amber sometimes contains animal or plant material which was caught up in the resin while it was still liquid. Whether a piece of amber has carried passengers with it or not, it is a perfect and beautiful time capsule bringing us life-forms from the distant past.

Nestling in the same cubby-hole is a heart-shaped piece of Purbeck stone bought when my son and I visited Swanage, a seaside town in Dorset, England. Purbeck stone was the predominant material used to build the villages and towns in the area. My small mottled grey and brown stone is a representative of this beautiful part of England.

As I mentioned earlier, people like to collect objects which represent the things that are important to them and this urge often seems to manifest itself very strongly when we are travelling to new locations. Places that we know we are unlikely to ever see again will effectively be comparable to past events and fictional worlds as soon as we leave the area. Although the location stills exists, our only access to it in the future will be through our memories, imagination and photographic records. Buying a souvenir, especially if it actually originates from there, helps us to feel that a part of the place will always be with us, even if we never physically visit it again. The Purbeck stone, although thousands of kilometres from its original home, has brought a trace of Dorset into my study and my life. I love knowing that an actual piece of England is sitting on my desk.

When I was in Britain I made a point of touching the natural elements of the land, such as the stonework in castle ruins, trunks of trees, and even the soil. I thought that if I didn't do this, it would theoretically be possible to spend weeks in a country and not actually touch it, apart from eating some locally grown food and drinking and bathing in the water. For example, the interiors of buildings, such as hotel rooms or lobbies, may be entirely made up of imported materials, even down to the sheets on the bed and the paint on the walls. Similarly, although we may walk for hours visiting various landmarks and attractions, we may only be feeling the earth or cobble-stoned streets through the soles of our shoes.

Two black-faced sheep figurines stare out at the world in wide-eyed innocence from another of the desk's cubby-holes. They look like a cartoonist's interpretation rather than showing any family resemblance to their woolly cousins in the fields, but they are all the cuter for it. Mum and Dad bought them for me in Bourton-On-The-Water, a quintessentially picturesque village in the Cotswolds. My son and I had visited there briefly a few weeks previously, the first English village that I had ever physically, rather than just imaginatively, been to. It lived up to all of my exceedingly high expectations of what such a place should be. It was as if we had stepped off the bus and into a "Miss Marple" or "Midsomer Murders" film shoot. Now having these two sheep who were born in the area sitting contentedly in their cubby-hole is a reminder of the sheer joy I felt on that day. Too often, reality proves to be a poor imitation of the idealised vision we have built up of people, places or events over a long period of time. When it is actually superior to the imagined version it is special indeed.

For me, the English countryside and villages had a very high ideal to live up to. I had been avidly imbibing their essence ever since childhood, when I first discovered Enid Blyton's "The Famous Five" adventure stories. Reading about the exploits of the four English children and their dog, all of whom appeared to have an enviable talent for unearthing mysteries and solving them, I was introduced to the delights of rural England. The first of these twenty one books was set in the early 1940's. By the 1960's much of what was described may no longer have even existed, but I was blissfully unaware of this at the time and relished the world it conjured up. I was soon an enthusiastic Anglophile. It is probably due to this early influence, that as an adult I have always felt the strong gravitational pull of detective stories set in Britain, especially those where much of the 'action' occurs in the countryside or small villages. Fortunately for the real-life residents and visitors of these areas reality usually differs markedly from fiction in certain aspects, as the world inside a crime novel is not all clotted cream teas and chocolate-box-pretty cottages. The body counts often reach alarming levels very quickly. In some tales, a simple walk outside after dark will almost guarantee a grisly end to the evening for the foolhardy nocturnal wanderer. Perhaps these victims don't read crime novels.

Visiting a country for the first time is an exciting experience, mainly because so much of what we are seeing is different to our usual environment, either in dramatic or very subtle ways. Even every-day items have their own slightly different versions of those we are familiar with. When this journey is to the soil from which our family tree grew over centuries, before a few branches broke off and floated to distant shores, another facet is added to our experience.

It is more than 90 years since the last of my direct ancestors packed their portmanteaus and set sail for the Antipodes. Despite this, Britain, for me, felt like visiting the home of relatives, ones I hadn't previously met but had heard lots of stories about over the years. Although just meeting for the first time I could immediately feel the emotional connection between us, and the awareness that we shared the same ancestry and cultural heritage. While England and Scotland still retained their exotic auras, with their promise of new discoveries and adventures at every turn, it almost felt as if I was discovering a part of "home" I hadn't previously visited. Rather than it taking any sense of adventure away from exploring a new locale, this perception actually enriched my experience considerably.

Yet another cubby-hole contains a ceramic teddy bear dressed in graduation gown and mortar board sitting on a pile of books, with Oxford written on the spine of the lowest. Oxford was a disappointment to me to a certain extent. I had always seen it depicted, or had interpreted it, as an entire city of beautiful historic stone buildings. Although many edifices did meet, and often exceeded, my assumptions, discovering that others were modern and in some cases also ugly was quite a shock. That's the thing about photos and movies, they can carefully edit out what doesn't fit the scene they want to portray, but reality has a very wide camera-angle.

In contrast, the magic of Edinburgh was that it not only lived up to expectations but went far beyond them. Before my visit I had been told that it was one of the beautiful cities of the world. Upon arriving, I discovered that it was also a city generous and secure enough to allow the fictional world to exist quite comfortably within its stone walls and cobbled streets.

Shortly before I returned from my virtual trip to Central Park, I had come across a website which sold souvenirs of New York. Not only can we now travel from the comfort of home, but we can buy souvenirs of these trips without stepping outside our front door. While idly browsing the virtual shelves my attention was briefly held by a New York City snow globe. For a moment I wondered whether purchasing it as a memento of my virtual trip would be whimsical or perhaps just weird. Before getting too far down that speculative path however, I remembered that I had not budgeted for travel expenses of any sort for this journey and quickly left the store, empty-handed.

Although often aspiring to, and achieving, high levels of tackiness, snow globes have managed to remain a popular type of souvenir over the years. Snow globes originated in France in the late 19th century and since this time have played a variety of roles. They have been used for advertising, souvenirs, religious gifts, and election campaigns, to name a few. Their quality ranges from the mass produced to finely crafted versions. Many have become collectibles, fetching prices far exceeding their original cost. Perhaps this longevity can be partly attributed to their ability to "enclose" their contents - whether a simple figure or a detailed scene - thereby creating a world in miniature. This ability would be particularly valuable for the souvenir and memento branches of the snow globe family, as the place, people or event depicted are securely ensconced within the dome. The dome represents the boundaries of this symbolic miniature world, keeping it inviolate from the outside environment. It is this ability - to allow its contents to remain complete within its protective sphere and not be randomly mixed with other outside elements - that gives the snow globe an advantage. Even if it was to sit on a shelf surrounded by a multitude of other objects, it retains its own identity. Its companions, unless similarly protected, lose a part of themselves to their shelf-mates' personalities.

Of course, snow globes don't have the monopoly on being able to create and maintain their own miniaturised worlds. Many other objects, dolls' houses for example - those designed for children as well as those more suited for adults – also have this useful talent. It is of no consequence to the dolls' house whether the style of the room it sits in is French Chateau or resembles an army bunker. It is quite capable of defending its own territory. The décor of each is firmly separated by the walls of the dolls' house, with no undesirable or embarrassing hybridisation of styles.

I imagine that dolls houses owe their enduring popularity to the intrinsic desire which many of us have, of creating a domestic environment which speaks to us, no matter whether it be the language of ultra-modernism, the Victorian era, or anything else. Even those who can afford to completely indulge their decorating tastes often only have one residence to play with. The passionate desires they may also have for Ancient Egyptian and Shabby Chic would thus have to remain unsatisfied. For them, and for those whose finances would not bear the strain of succumbing to even one of their furbishing fantasies, a dolls house is the perfect miniaturised version.

Opening a drawer of my desk I find a stack of cards marking my 50th birthday, which I celebrated a couple of months ago.

I don't really feel fifty, more like a concoction of different ages. Somewhere in my murky depths I'm still nineteen, although hopefully a lot wiser and more sensible than I actually was then. Many people long past the first flush of youth say they still feel very young deep down and can often pin-point a specific age. It seems that our "core" doesn't change much over time and what makes "us" feel like "us" stays essentially the same. They say 50 is the new 40, but on the physical health level for me, 50 is the new 80.

Although there can be many downsides to getting on a bit, such as less memory and increasingly creaky joints, it's certainly not all bad. Even though I'm still a walking anxiety attack some of the time, I feel much more self-assured than in my youth. I have a better sense of my own identity, whereas in my teens and twenties I felt hollow and lacking in direction. Judging from what I've read and heard, this is a natural progression for many people. As they get older they feel more aware of and comfortable with who they are, and calmer about life in general.

Even though I haven't worn well lately, and probably couldn't even be salvaged for spare parts, I feel grateful and privileged to have been able to celebrate my 50th birthday. A lot of people I have known along the way will never have that chance, dying long before reaching that milestone. If we still have enough health to get enjoyment out of life it seems churlish to complain about growing older.

There is a strange period of time between young adulthood and seriously old age where people are made to feel almost as if they are committing a serious social faux pas by growing older. People are often embarrassed to admit to being anywhere between their mid-thirties and eighty, as if they've somehow carelessly wandered away from their youth. After decades of creeping guiltily through the badlands of middle and early old age, the survivors who make it to their 80's and beyond are happy to reveal their advanced years. Old age seems to have a certain cachet attached to it. These people have managed, either by sheer luck or a combination of sensible management and good fortune, to out-live many of their contemporaries.

In the same drawer as my birthday cards I come across an old employment identity tag, a reminder of my last job. Finding it has provoked quite a few memories, from the very positive to the very painful. It is ironic that the photo on the card resembles a mug shot because at the time it was taken I was actually beginning to feel imprisoned within the job. At first I had thoroughly enjoyed it, despite the high workload and stress levels. Over time however, I realised that despite coping well with some aspects of the work, others were beginning to cause severe anxiety and depression. Despite this, I felt that I had too much invested in the job to resign and look for alternative employment. I had studied for years to gain the qualifications which originally helped me secure the position, and I had permanency with a state government department, which was not something to be discarded lightly. My qualifications were also not generic enough to transfer easily to an area outside the one I was currently employed in.

There are many types of prisons, not all of them visible to the naked eye. I was busy building one for myself in my head, convinced that I couldn't leave a job despite the fact that it was now seriously undermining my health. For many years Perth's minimum security prisons had no physical barriers stopping their inmates from simply wandering off, but the prisoners knew there would be serious penalties if they were foolish enough to try and escape their situation. I also had no physical restraints stopping me, but I believed that the consequences of making a dash for freedom might be worse than remaining where I was. (Long-term unemployment was my biggest fear.)

Many of us imprison ourselves by our self-doubt, not trusting in our ability to cope with making changes even when we know deep down that we should. Unlike the afore-mentioned minimum security prisoner who knows unequivocally what will happen if he leaves, we often don't know what the consequences will be if we act. This uncertainty can immobilise us. We are often tempted to remain within the current situation because a familiar environment, no matter how uncomfortable, can feel less intimidating than the unknown, however promising. This strategy can often backfire and it certainly did so in my case. Although it took a few more years to do so, eventually the stresses of the job contributed significantly to my current health situation. Sometimes when we let fear stop us escaping our self-imposed prisons, external circumstances then conspire to secure our release. Unfortunately this is often not in ways we would have wished for or anticipated. By opening the door and voluntarily stepping through it ourselves, rather than waiting to be dragged out, we have more chance of retaining control over our new situation.

After returning the I.D. card to the drawer, I take out and look through a folder of photos, a visual record of a brief time-out on Rottnest Island with my sister in 2007. Just off the coast, Rottnest could not have been more perfectly positioned and qualified to be an island holiday getaway if it had been specifically designed and built for the purpose. As always, during the three days we were there it kept its unspoken promise to induce high levels of relaxation and simple pleasure in its temporary residents. The island is home to a colony of quokkas, a very rare species of improbably cute marsupial. It is bordered by white sandy beaches and rocky inlets, and retains large areas of natural bushland. As well as its natural attributes there is a 'settlement' dotted with historic buildings, now used as shops and accommodation. There is also a total ban on private vehicles and domestic animals. With all of this bounty it is no surprise that Rottnest effortlessly weaves its magic over thousands of visitors each year.

Cycling and walking are the predominant ways of getting around the island, which encourages people to slow down and be more aware of their surroundings. The natural environment can create significant positive changes in our emotional state. When it teams up with a small, relatively undeveloped island which has embraced an unhurried lifestyle, its powers are formidable. Years often hurtle by between my visits to the island but each time, as soon as I venture onto its shores, its atmosphere of calm begins seeping into my marrow. Even on the couple of occasions many years ago when I arrived in a state of physical and emotional exhaustion, staggering onto the jetty like a ship-wreck survivor, the island was up to the challenge. Upon leaving, six or seven days later, I would be almost bouncing with energy, ready to return to the real world and all its demands.

If the level of difficulty of booking chalet accommodation during peak holiday periods is any indication, it would seem that many others have also succumbed to Rottnest's charms.

One of my desk drawers holds several notebooks, mostly unused, of varying dimensions and styles. The reasons for buying them at different times are now forgotten, but I would probably have earmarked them for jotting down some creative idea I wanted to develop. Perhaps it was simply that I can't resist the siren song of an attractively bound notebook. A couple of them have the beginnings of stories scribbled inside, temporarily abandoned but with the vague promise that I would return to them someday and help the various characters fulfil their fictional destinies.

New stationery is so enticing because the blank page allows us to believe that we are capable of creating great things. Until the first words are transferred from our imaginations to the page, there are potentially no limits to what can be created. From the moment we begin to fill the blank space the options become progressively fewer, as we commit to a certain direction. The struggle to be true to our vision plays out on the page, sometimes successfully, at other times not. Perhaps it is the unlimited potential of the pristine page that can sometimes make beginning a story so difficult. It feels almost like an act of vandalism to mark the paper with words that we fear will not prove worthy of having been released from the pen.

A few years ago I was keen to try writing a crime novel, but despite my enthusiasm I couldn't bring myself to sit down and put even the first sentence on paper. The ideas were in my head but they stubbornly refused to make the leap onto the page. Although I had previously written a number of short stories and poems, I hadn't attempted a full-length book since I was about ten years old. It had however, been a life-long goal to someday do so. I used all sorts of justifications to convince myself that my non-starting was valid, the main one being lack of time. Eventually I realised that I was too scared to begin, because once I did, I might find that I couldn't actually write after all. A major life goal was at stake, or so I believed. Because I was afraid of failing it was becoming a self-fulfilling prophecy. If fear stopped me from writing the book at all, I would have managed to fail without needing to put a single word down on paper. Making an attempt would give me some chance of success, no matter how small, of completing a readable work. Not making the attempt guaranteed failure, as the book had flatly refused to write itself. This belated realisation enabled me to finally start writing.

As it happened, my ideas for the plot ran out but I felt it had been a victory of sorts despite this, as I had actually had "a go" at it. It also allowed me to avoid the same mistake later on. Now when I have an idea, I don't become paralysed by the fear of it not working before I even get the first few sentences safely onto the page. In addition to this, the experience helped me realise what should have been obvious earlier. Even if I couldn't write this particular book at this time it did not mean I would not write one someday. I wondered why I had thought I needed to succeed at the first attempt.

In another of the drawers I find sheets of writing paper held together with a bulldog clip. Sometime during 2011, I again became inspired to try writing a novel and had got as far as creating brief resumes for the main characters, as well as knowing the major plot points. Many of the sheets of paper are covered in hastily scrawled, very rough outlines of scenes which would have been intended for insertion at various points throughout the story.

In the past, when reading books on how to write novels, I often read about authors who claimed that their characters would sometimes charge off in surprising directions. They would do and say things their creator had not anticipated, taking on a virtual life of their own. As fascinating as I found this idea, I didn't really believe it could happen as the authors described, thinking they were probably exaggerating a little. I was very surprised when I began working on my own embryonic novel to suddenly discover what they were referring to. Often when I was sitting watching television or reading, scenes would pop into my head, along with the relevant characters discussing or arguing about something. Although very helpful, it meant that I was constantly distracted from other activities, as I had to quickly write down the gist of what was happening before I forgot it. The characters from my previously attempted novel years earlier had been very passive, not bestirring themselves at all until being sharply prodded with my pen.

Now, looking through these abandoned notes from my second novel attempt, I saw that I had also made a start on writing the narrative but hadn't got very far. Reading through the first few pages, it reminded me that I had re-written the beginning quite a few times, although it was still not quite at the "final draft" stage. I had been very unsure how to proceed, having little confidence in my ability to write convincing scenes and dialogue or to juggle various plot lines. Usually I would write the first draft of a story from beginning to end without pausing to edit. This time, due to the lack of confidence, I had stayed safely at the beginning, constantly jostling and harassing the sentences

I had already managed to round up and capture. Although some authors do polish every sentence until it shines before moving onto the next, my preferred method is to write straight through with very minimal changes. I then return to the beginning to start the next of the many drafts it will go through. Having realised that I was once again becoming paralysed by fear, I had reminded myself that an unedited First Draft was supposed to be embarrassingly bad. It was almost a legal requirement. This had allowed me to move forward and, as expected, the next few pages were abysmal but I no longer minded.

Despite having overcome the fear of creating a woeful first draft, I stopped work on the story shortly afterwards. I felt that there were valid reasons for this, which I will explain later. I have an uneasy suspicion however, that perhaps I am not cut out to be a novelist. Some writers are capable of constantly dashing nimbly between non-fiction and fiction without breaking stride, while others attempting the same feat end up with a badly turned ankle, or worse. Unfortunately I seem to have unintentionally started a collection of barely begun novels. Here then is what could well be my total, life-long contribution to the world of published fiction, the much-edited first few pages of my latest attempt at a novel:

## TITLE: LOOKING FOR JILL

## PROLOGUE

*As she looked at the expressions on the faces of her three friends, which ranged from disbelief to shocked surprise, Jill felt an all-enveloping sense of panic. Had the decision to finally share her secret been the most misguided one of her life? She had lived with it alone for so long, why had she suddenly felt the need to tell them? She knew it would test the depth of these friendships, and the characters of these women she had known for so long. The moments, disguised as hours, passed in silence as her companions attempted to process the startling information they had just been given.*

## CHAPTER ONE

*Jill turned the T.V. on to the news channel and began eating the previous night's re-heated left-overs from the plate somewhat precariously balanced on her knees. As she watched the stories of violence and political scandals, which seemed to be repeated night after night with only the characters and locations changing, she thought how easily the habits of a life-time can be broken. Until a few months ago she would never have eaten dinner in front of the television, and almost never alone. Tonight the electronic voices were accentuating, rather than alleviating her feeling of aloneness. She wondered whether Dan and his Bitch were at that very moment enjoying a cosy dinner together in his new up-market inner city apartment. As Jill had derisively pointed out to her friends, Dan was managing his mid-life crisis with the style and efficiency he brought to almost everything he did. So far he was following the "Male Menopause-Dysfunctional Version" hand-book to the letter, replacing his wife with a much younger specimen, (already thoroughly tested for suitability before making the switch), buying a convertible sports car to show her off in, and moving into a trendy bachelor-pad.*

*As soon as she had finished her meal, Jill washed the few dishes in the sink and resolved to make the most of her evening alone, instead of letting the anger towards her ex-husband cloud everything, as it too often did. It had been a particularly difficult day at work, and if she didn't find a way to de-compress, she didn't know if she could cope with going in tomorrow. Not that she expected a repeat of today's events any time soon. It wasn't often that a client, high on amphetamines, started throwing chairs around the reception area and tried to break the security screen to get to the receptionist cowering behind it. Luckily everyone was still physically in one piece at the end of the drama, but unfortunately the same couldn't be said for their nerves, which were in shreds.*

*Deciding that getting out of her own head and into someone else's would be a good way to relax, Jill returned to the living room. Turning the television off, she picked a book up off the coffee table that she was part-way through reading and made herself comfortable on the sofa. Titled, "On The Run" it was a light-hearted debut novel by a local author. Jill was not usually very adventurous in trying out new authors she hadn't heard of. Over the years too many of her dollars had been spent supporting writers who had missed their calling as butchers, if their enthusiastic slaughtering of the English language was any indication. She had come across this book by chance, having been in a bookshop at the time the author was doing a signing. For reasons still unknown to her, Jill impetuously decided to join the queue of three or four people. Minutes later she was leaving the store with a signed copy of a book she barely remembered the name of as soon as it was in the carry-bag. She had caught herself doing quite a lot of that recently, impulse buying of whatever happened to be close by when the urge hit. It was quite unnerving, as, although she enjoyed a good shopping spree as much as the next person, she had always prided herself on being sensible about her choices. Jill tried to reassure herself that she was just indulging in "retail therapy" during a stressful period of her life, and her normal habits would return when they thought it was the right time.*

*Luckily buying "On The Run" proved to be one of Jill's successful impulse purchases, and as she escaped into the humorous world between the pages, her real-world worries, temporarily de-moralised at suddenly being ignored, began to loosen their grip. As Jill marked her place with a bookmark and put the book down an hour later, she slowly looked around the room she was in. Unlike the book's main character, who was very comfortable in her surroundings, Jill felt as if she was living in someone else's house. For that matter, she thought, she also felt as if she was living someone else's life. It was now three weeks since the sale had been finalised and she and the twins had moved in, the real estate agent there with the keys and congratulating them on their new home. She didn't tell him there was nothing good about successfully finding a new house, no matter how suitable, when all they really wanted was to be able to keep their old one.*

. . .

I had decided to stop work on the book as I didn't feel confident enough to explore the issues I wanted the novel to focus on. The subject that I had intended to address was due, indirectly, to some of my own childhood experiences. As a child I was extremely shy and because of this was targeted mercilessly by bullies throughout my school years. This made me feel somewhat of an outsider and inferior to so-called normal people, and took decades to recover from. As a child we believe others' assessments of us and as I had constantly been told by some of my fellow students that I was somehow deficient, I ended up thinking they must be right. After leaving school I thought such experiences would be left behind me, wrongly assuming that systematic bullying was confined to the school yard. When it happened again, this time in the workplace, I was in my forties. Although distressing, both to experience personally and to witness happening to others, I could clearly see that the perpetrators, not the victims, were the inadequate specimens of the human race. These bullies were supposedly intelligent, employed in very responsible positions, yet were obviously so insecure and dysfunctional that they felt compelled to lash out in an attempt to bolster their own self-esteem.

Although I had long known that bullies were the ones with the personality issues, not the victims, I had only believed it at an intellectual level, so the wounds from childhood were still not completely healed and were prone to become inflamed from time to time. When confronted with the issue again as an adult I suddenly knew the truth at an emotional level, which was very liberating. Knowing that something is true is only powerful when we also feel that truth.

Perhaps it is because of my childhood experiences and the damage it caused, that I have always felt strongly about the issue of various types of people being harassed for no legitimate reason. In my case it had been simply because I was an unusually introverted child. When I began thinking about writing a novel I knew I wanted to include someone from a minority group that has had to deal with society's prejudice simply because they don't fit neatly into the "mainstream". I wanted to write about an issue that readers would know little or nothing about. Too often ignorance leads to fear and then hatred and intolerance, so hopefully knowledge would lead to understanding and acceptance.

The transgender population is a group which until recently has been largely ignored or ostracised in our society, and is only now receiving occasional positive attention. I decided to make one of the main characters of my novel transgender. Knowing only a little about the subject, I turned to the internet for information regarding this community.

One of the reasons I decided to stop work on my novel was that I had begun having serious doubts about my ability to write it well. Having now read extensively on the subject, I knew that the transgender community varies widely in their identifications with gender and don't fit neatly into one homogeneous group. I was worried that by trying to create a fictional character with the intention of showing my readers the experience of a transgender person, I may get it wrong and hinder rather than help. Because relatively few people in the wider community know much about transgender issues, I felt that anyone who addressed the subject had a moral responsibility to portray it accurately and not inadvertently add to the myths and misconceptions already out there. I could have simply dropped the idea of creating a transgender character and continued my novel without her. However, because she had already got into my head and begun interacting with the other characters I felt the story would not properly recover if she was forced to leave.

Sitting on top of my maybe-someday-novel notes is a small, attractively decorated papier-mache box. There always seems a promise vaguely hinted at by boxes, that they could be the keepers of exotic treasures or dangerous secrets. Mostly we find that they were bluffing, but the prospect of opening a box with unknown or forgotten contents usually arouses our curiosity. Who can blame Pandora for succumbing to her natural curiosity and unintentionally causing havoc by opening that most infamous of boxes?

A box is seemingly a mere construction, often of cardboard, that simply encloses a certain area of space. Putting an object inside this contained space however, often endows it with a higher prestige than it enjoyed before it was confined. For example, quality jewellery is usually presented to its lucky recipient in a box, rather than simply wrapped in paper. Expensive goods are often lavishly boxed, befitting and increasing their status. Perhaps this perceived improvement in prominence happens because once an object is safely ensconced inside a box it is separated from its everyday surroundings. It now has centre-stage in its own environment.

The "box" concept isn't just used for objects. In a similar way, people are often contained separately from their compatriots as a sign of prestige. Many sporting and cultural venues for example have relatively luxurious "box seats" for those of higher means or status, separating them from the rigours of sitting elbow to elbow with strangers. Offices often have enclosed spaces in which they keep their senior staff while the rest jostle for room in open-plan areas.

Exclusive spaces and the rightful claim to them, whether the claimant be a diamond necklace or a company executive, are coveted to a large extent for their associations with worth and prestige in the eyes of others, as well as for their more obvious comfort value.

The "container as status symbol" concept is most evident in the homes people live in. Many people aspire, and often strain themselves financially, to buy the fanciest "box" possible in which to display themselves. Luxury cars are another and conveniently mobile display box. Leaders of countries are given residence in high quality display boxes as a tangible affirmation of their power and status. One of the most notable examples being The White House, where the American President lives for the duration of his Presidential term. Sadly, at the opposite end of the spectrum the importance of having one's own box is also illustrated by the low status of the homeless in society. People who can't lay claim to even the most basic of private containers, even if it be only a virtually derelict bed-sit, are, usually unfairly, amongst those accorded the least respect by their fellow citizens.

Islands, although obviously not boxes, share some of their attributes. An island is a self-contained space, the water surrounding it becoming the walls which remove it from the wider world. The smaller the island, the greater the sense of separation and the impression of being in a unique environment. Many islands are transformed into holiday resorts, creating their own distinctive community and rules, which dramatically reinforces the detachment from the everyday world. One of the ultimate status symbols for the mega-wealthy is owning their own island, an open-aired display box of the finest quality.

Some women are obsessed with finding and owning the perfect handbag, humble containers which virtually become life-support systems once their owners leave the house. I enjoy a good handbag too, but my obsession is more focussed on its larger cousin, the travel bag. The quest for the perfect travel companion, luggage-wise, stems I think, from some of the same instinct that motivates us to search for our ideal home. In a home we look for something in which we can comfortably hold our worldly goods and which feels like our little corner of the world, our tiny toehold on the planet. When travelling, we leave the security of home behind, and it is just us and the few possessions we have stuffed into our luggage. The travel bag temporarily becomes the container of every object we have and rely upon, as the rest of our possessions could be half a planet away and may as well not exist at that moment. At the end of a day's sightseeing we may be returning to an unfamiliar room, just the latest in a constantly changing stream of them. Our luggage and its precious contents will be the familiar connection to home that stops us feeling totally adrift. Just as a home is more than simply shelter, so too our luggage is more than just something to transport our belongings from one location to another.

Although I've never managed to do so, I have always liked the idea of travelling with as little luggage as possible, as less possessions equals more freedom and spontaneity to go wherever the whim takes you. One man I heard of a while ago had taken this idea to the extreme, apparently very successfully. He didn't have any luggage at all, but simply stowed his few necessities such as changes of clothes, toiletries and documents in large pockets on his jacket and pants. He said this method of travelling was very liberating. He didn't have to wait at airport luggage carousels and he could easily jump on and off local transport, as well as various other benefits. One disadvantage was that sometimes customs officials got suspicious when they saw that he was travelling without luggage on international flights. Although I admire his creativity, I couldn't imagine being able to travel without a day pack at the very least. The only downside to my current journey around my room is that I couldn't use it as an excuse to go luggage shopping.

Exploring another desk drawer I find some unused postcards, acquired on a very enjoyable 9-day cruise from Perth to Sydney that I took with Mum late last year. Mum's health was also at a low point, having not yet fully recovered from the aftermath of a viral illness, so it was the ideal type of holiday for us. We could do as much or as little as we chose to, depending on our energy level at any given time.

The cruise did wonders for my emotional health and put me into the right frame of mind to begin the journey around my study soon afterwards. Without having been away from it for awhile I couldn't have gathered up enough enthusiasm to explore it. Before this holiday I hadn't been out of Perth's clutches for over four years, and had been feeling like a virtual prisoner in my restricted environment. Because I hadn't stepped out of my normal routine at all for so long, I had lost perspective on small, everyday issues we all face, with my stress levels inevitably rising because of it.

Usually one of the first questions to come up when meeting people for the first time is "What do you do for a living?", but on the ship this was replaced by "Are you enjoying the trip?", "Is this your first cruise?" and similar enquiries. In the relatively self-contained on-board environment people's everyday stories weren't the highest priority. The lives we usually led were largely left behind on the dock and we were now in a different world of holidays and relaxation. It was as if we were actors on a new film set and our previous roles were much less important than our current one. I assume this change of focus isn't exclusive to cruises, but would be common amongst all types of non-business travel groups. People in holiday mode are interested in the travel experiences of their companions, sharing information relevant to their current circumstances. They don't want or need to be emotionally re-connected to the everyday work-life world.

The following passage is De Maistre's, in which he makes an interesting claim and recounts an entertaining anecdote:

*"I put on my travelling-coat, after having examined it with a complacent eye; and forthwith resolved to write a chapter ad-hoc, that I might make it known to the reader.*

*The form and usefulness of these garments being pretty generally known, I will treat specially of their influence upon the minds of travellers.*

*My winter travelling-coat is made of the warmest and softest stuff I could meet with. It envelops me entirely from head to foot, and when I am in my arm-chair, with my hands in my pockets, I am very like the statue of Vishnu one sees in the pagodas of India.*

*You may, if you will, tax me with prejudice when I assert the influence a traveller's costume exercises upon its wearer. At any rate I can confidently affirm with regard to this matter, that it would appear to me as ridiculous to take a single step of my journey round my room in uniform, with my sword at my side, as it would to go forth into the world in my dressing-gown. Were I to find myself in full military dress, not only should I be unable to proceed with my journey, but I really believe I should not be able to read what I have written about my travels, still less to understand it.*

*Does this surprise you? Do we not every day meet with people who fancy they are ill because they are unshaven, or because someone has thought they have looked poorly, and told them so? Dress has such influence upon men's minds that there are valetudinarians who think themselves in better health than usual when they have on a new coat and well-powdered wig. They deceive the public and themselves by their nicety about dress, until one finds some fine morning they have died in full fig, and their death startles everybody.*

*And in the class of men among whom I live, how many there are who, finding themselves clothed in uniform, firmly believe they are officers, until the unexpected appearance of the enemy shows them their mistake. And more than this, if it be the king's good pleasure to allow one of them to add to his coat a certain trimming, he straightway believes himself to be a general, and the whole army gives him the title without any notion of making fun of him! So great an influence has a coat upon the human imagination!*

*The following illustration will show still further the truth of my assertion.*

*It sometimes happened that they forgot to inform the Count de ----- some days beforehand of the approach of his turn to mount guard. Early one morning, on the very day on which this duty fell to the Count, a corporal awoke him, and announced the disagreeable news. But the idea of getting up there and then, putting on his gaiters, and turning out without having thought about it the evening before, so disturbed him that he preferred reporting himself sick and staying at home all day. So he put on his dressing-gown, and sent away his barber. This made him look pale and ill, and frightened his wife and family. He really did feel a little poorly.*

*He told everyone he was not very well, partly for the sake of appearances, and partly because he positively believed himself to be indisposed. Gradually the influence of the dressing-gown began to work. The slops he was obliged to take upset his stomach. His relations and friends sent to ask after him. He was soon quite ill enough to take to his bed.*

*In the evening Dr Ranson found his pulse hard and feverish, and ordered him to be bled next day. If the campaign had lasted a month longer, the sick man's case would have been past cure.*

*Now, who can doubt about the influence of travelling-coats upon travellers, if he reflect that poor Count de ----- thought more than once that he was about to perform a journey to the other world for having inopportunely donned his dressing-gown in this?*

*(De Maistre, A Journey Round My Room, p. 132 - 136)*

# CHAPTER SEVEN

Before I explore my roll-top desk further, I will re-trace my steps back to the bookcase. There are some residents who haven't yet been introduced, which gives me the perfect excuse to return to my collection again. I never last long on any type of journey without feeling the need to read something, or at least have a book close by. Before delving into the shelves however, my attention makes a brief stop on the top of my bookcase, where I see an ancient black manual typewriter. The machine is in virtually perfect condition despite being made sometime in the 1940's. It's only obvious flaw being that it is merely a figment of my imagination. This typewriter does, or at least did exist, but unfortunately the last time I saw it in its physical manifestation was in an antique shop on the south coast.

I was fascinated by it as soon as I saw it, wondering about its history and speculating on all the dramatic stories it may have collaborated on over the years. I feel again a pang of regret at not having bought it when I saw it 24 years ago. At the time however, it was not appropriate, costing more than I could afford to spend on what was really just an ornament, as I was unlikely to use it.

As I imagine the typewriter on my bookcase I know the image won't survive any sudden movements, reaching out a hand to touch its shiny black surface will send it retreating into the recesses of my mind. Nevertheless it is fun seeing it again, no matter how brief the virtual re-union proves to be.

Shifting my gaze and breaking the illusion, I do a visual rummage through the bookshelves to find those volumes that have so far gone unmentioned in my travel notes. One of these is Henry David Thoreau's "Walden", an example of a Classic that lives up to the term. The book is an account of Thoreau's experiences and ideas while living in a wooden cabin in the American woods in 1845. He built the cabin himself and grew much of his own food during this time.

Although "Walden" is now a classic of literature it hardly even registered on the public's awareness when it was originally published in 1854. This was presumably because Thoreau was a deep thinker and didn't blindly accept that the way society was constructed was the only way it could be. He could see beneath the shallow surface of tradition and most of the people of the time probably couldn't understand what he was saying. Some of the most recognised quotes we see today are from the mind and pen of Thoreau, many of them quite inspirational. It is a pity that Walden didn't get the recognition it deserved during his lifetime.

Earlier I talked about how books sometimes enter our lives and have profound effects on us. Two books which have unequivocally altered my life are "The Power of Now" and "A New Earth", written by Eckhart Tolle. These two volumes have pride of place in my bookcase and have been read repeatedly.

Tolle is a spiritual teacher and although he refers to a number of religions and traditions at times, his message is not allied to any specific one. One of his major themes is explaining how to overcome destructive thought patterns and attitudes, as well as the importance of living life in the present rather than being burdened by the past and fearing the future. As Tolle says, his message is not new.

Having suffered from severe clinical depression for many years, it suddenly disappeared after reading "The Power of Now" a number of times over a period of months.

(This happened during my previously referred-to week in Brisbane.) This life-changing event occurred almost eight years ago and since this time I have had only a few very short-lived recurrences of depression. These are usually successfully banished by reading and practising Tolle's teachings, as well as distracting myself with enjoyable or creative activities. Writing, reading, or watching Magnum episodes, for example.

A newcomer to my bookcase, Virginia Woolf's "A Room of One's Own", is another Classic which I feel deserves its acclaimed status. Over the years I have heard Woolf referred to many times, especially in relation to this book, but had never read any of her work. Shortly before beginning my journey around my study, I came upon yet another reference to Virginia Woolf and "A Room of One's Own" in a book I was reading, so I finally decided it was time I experienced this literary icon for myself.

I like the way authors refer to other writers whose work they respect and either incidentally or specifically encourage others to read them. It's akin to being at a party and the person we are speaking to introducing us to one or more of the other guests. These new acquaintances will often then introduce us to someone else, and so it goes. Unlike a real party, this virtual one has the advantage that the guests still being alive is not a prerequisite. This is not to say that the author we are introduced to will necessarily be to our liking. Some of the introductions I've had have been very disappointing and I regretted having taken up the offer of a meeting. Fortunately, another advantage to this virtual gathering is that we can throw our new acquaintance down in disgust and walk away if we strongly dislike them. This type of behaviour is usually frowned upon in polite circles.

Although some introductions are better left unmade, others prove to be very worthwhile and a new friend is made.

Even a book which has been labelled a Classic, or one with multiple awards in its resume, isn't necessarily worth reading. There seems to be no definitive correlation between official accolades and quality, these two factors sometimes intersecting, but quite often not even coming close. It often happens that if a book or author is celebrated by an award, or an influential section of the literary world approves them, others automatically follow the verdict, not stopping to consider whether they themselves actually think it's good. Thus a reputation spreads, sometimes undeservedly, and those who secretly think the work's rightful place is in a shredder are afraid to say so, concerned that they've simply missed the point of the book. Perhaps the story "The Emperor's New Clothes" should be required reading for everyone, which may encourage people to think for themselves rather than blindly follow the herd.

One book I read recently, after seeing it referred to by numerous other authors over the years, was supposedly a pioneering masterpiece of its genre. I was surprised and disappointed, after so many recommendations about its cleverness, when I found it quite unreadable. The story was crammed so full of long passages describing either people or places in minute detail that it was hard to follow. Every time the story looked set to gather some momentum it was stopped in its tracks by another bout of descriptive diarrhoea. Many of the sentences were clumsily put together, with repetitions of words and obvious structural faults. I seriously doubt that it would have found a publisher if it had been written and submitted now.

Obviously that is my subjective opinion, but I suspect the book's stature in the literary realm is due to it being given high praise by a few of the literati of the day who had influence, and its reputation was born. Sadly, if all of the alleged literary masterpieces were gathered together, it would involve sifting through a lot of dross to get to the gems scattered amongst them.

Of course, I realise many won't agree with my opinions and personal favourites, as each of us has our own subjective literary tastes. But the important point is that we should ensure that our opinions are in fact our own, based on personal reading experience and not simply what we have heard from others and feel obliged to agree with.

Virginia Woolf's "A Room of One's Own" was written in 1928 and although aimed at women of that time, is still very relevant to today's readers. Woolf conveys her profound insights and ideas to her readers in a poetic writing style that would make it a pleasure to read even if her subject matter was banal.

Woolf talks about how it was virtually impossible for women to become writers before the eighteenth century. Women's lives were almost never recorded before this time, as the concerns and exploits of men were the only ones considered worth writing about. At one point Woolf describes the fate of Shakespeare's imaginary sister, assuming that she had been as equally gifted as her brother. Not surprisingly, it doesn't end well for her.

According to Woolf even as late as the nineteenth century in England the daunting material difficulties which faced women who wanted to write, such as lack of money and having a space of her own, were not nearly as bad as the immaterial. Woolf said that male literary geniuses such as

Keats and Flaubert often had to deal with the world not caring about their writing. For women however, the world reacted with hostility rather than indifference and actively discouraged them from attempting anything intellectual.

Reading "A Room of One's Own" reminds me just how lucky we are in our society today, in being free to pursue whatever creative endeavours we wish. Not having the economic resources and "a room of one's own" in which to be creative are still obstacles for many of us, but men too face the same challenges. At least now, society itself doesn't mock or abuse women for wanting to write, paint, compose or do anything else creative. Some individuals may still be subject to the scepticism of their own family or friends, but this is easier to ignore when their attitudes are not reflected in the wider world. At the time Woolf wrote "A Room of One's Own" there was still a great deal of sexism, with men constantly claiming that women were intellectually inferior to the male of the species.

Woolf delivered a speech to a group of young women at Girton College, Cambridge in 1928 and "A Room of One's Own" grew out of this. Towards the end of the lecture she urged her audience to go forth and join the ranks of the world's authors, and to write about all sorts of subjects, no matter what they might be. Woolf also told them that it was vitally important that they wrote what they themselves wanted to write, and not simply what they thought would earn accolades from others.

If Woolf were able to visit the earthly realm of 2012, I think she would be pleased with the rich and varied results of women having put pen to paper over the past eighty three years since she made that speech. Once women were given the chance they seized it wholeheartedly, and the world of literature has benefited enormously since they've taken their rightful place alongside their male counterparts.

The Australian author I mentioned earlier, Miles Franklin, wrote an entertaining and thought-provoking sequel to "My Brilliant Career", titled "My Career Goes Bung". Franklin wrote this in 1902 and made a number of unsuccessful attempts to have it published. Decades later she made considerable revisions to the manuscript and it was published in 1946, when she was sixty six years old.

"My Career Goes Bung" is a novel which also explores the issue Woolf addressed - that of women being actively discouraged from writing.

Franklin's fictional heroine experienced the hostility of the conservative society of the day, which believed that it was unfeminine to write books. A woman's role was to marry, defer to her husband in all important matters, and provide him with children. Women who did not conform to this constricted life-path were considered man-haters and unnatural.

Franklin was one of Australia's early advocates of women's rights, using her intelligence and skill with the pen in an attempt to prise people's narrow world-view a little wider. In common with pioneers of any ilk it required great courage for Woolf, Franklin and others like them, to work at getting justice and an even playing field for women. They risked ridicule, open hostility and the condemnation of society in doing so. It was disturbing how even some women, the very group these early feminists were trying to help, would join in with the attacks on them, being too afraid or brainwashed to want the existing state of affairs disrupted. Many people, it would seem, are frightened of change even if it has the potential to be considerably better afterwards.

Although many men of the early and mid 20th century were firmly entrenched in their cosy bastions of power and had no intention of relinquishing any ground at all, there were others who could see the injustices of the system. Without the support of these fair-minded men who wanted their mothers, sisters, wives and daughters to have the same rights they themselves enjoyed, the various women's movements of the 20th century could not have succeeded. Any group that is weaker in some crucial way than its oppressors, whether it be physically, economically, fewer in number, or whatever the circumstances, needs allies within the ranks of the dominant group. Without them they cannot hope to overthrow the existing system.

As I read "My Career Goes Bung" I thought how relevant and comforting this book would have been to me if I had come across it in my childhood or teenage years. Growing up in the 1960's and 70's in rural Australia, I was very aware of the glaring imbalance between the rights of males and females, but I had no idea that women had actually written about this issue. Franklin's story and her fictional heroine would have affected the lives of many women and girls when it was first published. Some of her readers may have gone on to join the ranks of the feminist movement which radically altered the social landscape of the later part of the 20th century.

After reading Virginia Woolf's "A Room of One's Own" I was keen to learn more about this fascinating woman who wielded her pen like a magic wand over the page. Her personal story is a tragic one. Woolf was both blessed with creative genius and cursed with serious mental illness, bouts of which plagued her throughout her life. Tragically her illness would eventually defeat her. Woolf drowned herself at the age of 59. As well as her health issues she lost many family members and friends through illness, war and suicide. Despite serious challenges Woolf managed to not only carry on, for a long time at least, but to also create a body of work that would make her one of the literary names of the 20th century.

Whatever their arena, individuals who manage to achieve their goals despite daunting obstacles are inspirational, as they show us what is possible. In both fiction and non-fiction the most interesting characters are those who have significant challenges to deal with, either through their own personalities or their external circumstances. If the character has no flaws or problems and glides smoothly through life getting everything they desire, they are of no interest to us because that is not reality as we know it. They have nothing to teach us.

When researching transgender issues for my would-be novel last year, I ordered off the internet a book that is part memoir, part informative. It is titled "Transgender Explained – For Those Who Are Not", and written by Joanne Herman, an American transgender woman. This book is an informative mixture of facts, and Herman's personal account of her transition from male to female bodied. Herman covers a wide range of issues that transgender people often have to deal with, including shocking facts about the violence and wide-ranging discrimination committed against them. Because of the intolerance much of society has towards them many transgender people conceal their true identities, fearing for their physical safety, employment security or a multitude of other reasons.

Herman has spent a lot of her time and energy explaining transgender issues to people in the hope that increasing their knowledge will remove their prejudices. She is an admirable woman who has had the courage to take the risk of being "out" in order to help others.

# CHAPTER EIGHT

Journeying back to my roll-top desk my gaze is caught by the gimlet eye of my small Swarovski crystal hedgehog, a 50th birthday present from my sister. As I admire its beauty and think of its real-life counterparts it reminds me how enriched humanity is by having other creatures to share the planet with. What a Spartan existence it would be if humans were the only species to interact with and enjoy.

Quite apart from their functional purposes and the pleasure they give us, humanity can be elevated emotionally and morally by its relationship with animals. We have creatures other than our own species to care for, protect and learn from. One attribute we could emulate is to live more in the present moment. Unfortunately for these creatures who have to share the planet with us, we humans too often fall short of being the protectors and custodians that we should be. It is sobering to think that humans benefit from having animals around, but most of the planet's inhabitants would be far healthier if our species didn't exist.

Sitting next to my hedgehog is another Swarovski crystal ornament which, if we overlook some blatant design modifications, could lay claim to belonging to the equine family. The hedgehog's companion is a rocking horse, complete with silver saddle and a wonderfully old-fashioned air.

Many Victorian-era families with the means to do so would have stabled rocking horses in their children's nurseries. These toys were the equivalent of our modern-day pedal cars for today's children, allowing them to play-act mastery of what would later be their main mode of transportation. Luckily the rocking horse has not yet become an endangered species, despite its real-life inspiration now being retired from essential transport duty. We still rely on horses for various leisure pursuits so they have remained connected to us. This continuing connection has presumably been the factor that has saved the rocking horse from banishment to total obscurity. Sadly, although a wide variety of lesser-breeds are still easily acquired, the thoroughbreds of the species - the finely crafted wooden specimens - are now relatively hard to find.

I was lucky enough to own a horse during part of my childhood and my hoofed companion Mike, and I, spent many hours travelling along the sandy tracks on the family farm. He also transported me far beyond the property's boundaries. With Mike's help and my imagination, fuelled by having watched countless Westerns on T.V., we galloped fearlessly across prairies and deserts, or sedately set off across country to explore distant territories. Although it is more than thirty five years since I rode Mike, as I look at my tiny crystal rocking horse I can again remember the exhilaration of feeling his power and speed, the creak of the saddle and the smell of his horsy sweat as we entered into a world of our own.

Angled into a corner of the desk-top is a silver-framed photo of my grandparents, mother and aunt, which was taken sometime in 1941. Two more children missed out on this photo shoot as they were yet to make their debut appearances into the family.

My grandmother was a very gentle, kind woman and this is captured in the black and white image, but it was beyond the photo's capabilities to also show how courageous she was. As a young woman she saved the lives of two teenagers at the risk of her own. While spending the day at a popular swimming spot on the Swan River, Grandma noticed two girls quite a distance from shore who were in serious trouble. She swam out and grabbed hold of them, but was soon fearing that all three of them were about to drown. In their panic the girls were unwittingly pulling her down with them. Grandma said later that at this point she heard a loud male voice in her head telling her to "kick your legs". She did so, and managed to get them all safely to shore. Considering that Grandma was only a petite 5'2" or 155cm, she must have somehow tapped into a reserve of superhuman strength for the occasion.

Granddad, smartly dressed in his air force uniform in the photo, was a very conservative personality, even compared to his contemporaries. Because of this it was quite a surprise when one of his daughters gave him a teddy bear for his 80th birthday. His reaction to this could have gone in any direction, but his daughter's creativity in the gift-giving department paid off. Granddad was delighted and treasured the teddy for the rest of his life.

Even though we assume we know those close to us, they are often capable of surprises and we can't always automatically predict their reactions to events. Although we need to be able to count on predictable behaviours to a large extent, how dull it would be if people didn't occasionally act outside their perceived characters.

Also sitting on my desk-top is a stick of sealing wax. Keeping it company is a stamp indented with a depiction of an open book and a feather quill standing in an inkpot. Despite initially not knowing of a single practical use I would have for such items, I was entranced as soon as I discovered them in a delightful Sydney shop tucked inside the historic Victoria Building. I came across them during the cruise Mum and I took last year. My poor health meant that my previous employment path was now and would forever be closed to me, so prior to this trip I had resolved to seriously apply myself to my writing and see where it led me. Whether I failed miserably or succeeded spectacularly was not as important as finally following the direction I had felt drawn to from childhood. As I examined these humble-looking objects on their shelf in the shop I thought that they were symbolic of this resolve and that they could be of great practical use after all. I felt that buying and owning them would be a powerful affirmation to myself that "Yes, I am a Writer." Hopefully they will earn their keep and remind me of that when fear and self-doubt pay their inevitable, numerous visits in the future.

For De Maistre, quills, ink and sealing wax were not simply symbolic, but the essentials of his craft. He writes:

*"Upon opening the first drawer to the left, we find an inkstand, paper of all kinds, pens ready mended, and sealing-wax; all which set the most indolent person longing to write."* (De Maistre, A Journey Round My Room, p. 100)

Although pencils had been invented when De Maistre wrote his book, this excerpt suggests he used quill and ink, which were the predominant writing tools at the time. The ball-point pen had not yet even appeared in writer's fantasies and the first truly effective fountain pens were still years away. The patience of De Maistre and others who did a lot of writing in the days when the quill ruled the written word was admirable, as it would have been slow work. The quill points wore out quickly too, so had to be regularly re-shaped with a pen-knife. Once they were beyond repair a new quill needed to be plucked from the nearest slow-moving goose.

Opening a desk drawer I discover my much beloved and battered yellow toy jeep, nestled amongst notepads and various writing accessories. The small metal jeep is one of my few remaining childhood toys, and my most precious. Many of my clearest memories of this time are of my siblings and me playing in the sand on our farm, with our assortment of matchbox vehicles and plastic figures.

I keep the jeep parked in a drawer rather than on display somewhere. On the infrequent occasions I come across it I am immediately transported into the world of my childhood, with its atmosphere and sentiments semi-intact. If I were to see it constantly, it would, although still treasured, become just another of the objects in my day-to-day existence. It would soak up the ambience of today, rather than being a portal back into childhood.

Looking at the toy, I think about the phenomenon of school re-unions and the reasons for their existence. They provide good settings for television shows and movies, where their purpose is to allow everyone to boast to their schoolmates about how successful they have become. For most people however, perhaps there is another, more modest reason. Seeing people from the past for the first time since that era is a very powerful trigger for re-creating the atmosphere of that period of our lives. When we see people from our past regularly, they travel with us through time, staying part of our present rather than becoming a figure in our personal history. Unless we actively get nostalgic with them about the times of yore, they don't automatically transport us back. To do that, we need people who have figuratively speaking been kept in a drawer and who, when taken out, convey us into the past with them for a short while.

Often by returning to locations that we haven't visited for many years, it's possible to discover our former selves waiting there for us. While holidaying in Brisbane years ago I had a surprise encounter. Standing in a park in the centre of the city and looking up at the town hall I suddenly felt as if my nineteen year old self was there with me. Instead of seeing the towering sandstone building and its surrounds with forty two year-old eyes, I was looking at it from my teenage viewpoint with all her feelings, attitudes and fears. The intensity of the impression was uncomfortable as the nineteen year-old's perspective I was now experiencing had been very troubled.

I sometimes think that in years to come when my future self looks back at the incumbent me she might be gnashing her teeth in frustration about my judgement on important decisions and general woolly-headedness. It could be helpful if we were able to tap into the wisdom of our older selves, but then again, we might find that they're simply tiresome know-it-alls.

By sheer chance, while wandering fairly aimlessly around the labyrinthine corridors of the internet, I tripped over the following literary nugget. It is a quote by Charles Dickens, and I think it fits perfectly here:

*"For who can wonder that man should feel a vague belief in tales of disembodied spirits wandering through those places which they once dearly affected, when he himself, scarcely less separated from his old world than they, is forever lingering upon past emotions and bygone times, and hovering, the ghost of his former self, about the places and people that warmed his heart of old?" (Charles Dickens, from 'Master Humphrey's Clock'.)*

CHAPTER NINE

Moving on from my desk I reach the doorway, and the end of my journey. When I began I hoped it would be worthwhile, although exactly how I didn't know, as travel often rewards us in unexpected ways. One of the significant benefits of this experience has been that, as often happens with more conventional journeys, while in the throes of my travels I wasn't stressing out about the everyday issues of life. Each time I entered my study I became focused on exploring my environment. Writing about my discoveries became a meditation of sorts, going into the "zone", totally absorbed in getting my perceptions and thoughts down on paper. I had forgotten just how powerful creativity can be in shutting off the outside world, and it was a timely reminder.

Before beginning this journey I had serious doubts as to whether I had the physical and mental stamina to complete it at this point in time. I felt very motivated to start some sort of writing project but thought it might have to be put on hold for awhile. I did have to tailor my travels to suit my energy levels. Some days a mere half-hour in my study was all I was fit for. Sometimes, due to inclement health conditions I couldn't travel at all but stayed home, ensconced on the couch in a fog of exhaustion. On other days I would spend two to three hours, broken into small chunks of time, happily engrossed in my explorations.

Just as I had been ready to embark on the journey around my room, with my pen virtually poised over the paper to begin recording my experiences, my sister told me about something she had serendipitously come across in a magazine. A group of artists had set themselves a challenge:

to do 30 paintings in 30 days. I liked the concept and thought that I could give myself a similar challenge, but instead of becoming immersed in paint and canvas it would be in ink and paper. Although I was eager to begin my book, the task I had set myself was rather daunting. A daily quota sounded like a good way of getting through the early days of the Project. Mindful that it would be counter-productive to aim too high, I challenged myself to write a minimum of 350 words every day for 30 days. Because it was only the first draft the writing wouldn't need to be at all polished. The words could tumble out of my pen as rowdy and uncouth as they wished. As long as they formed a basically coherent sentence they would be counted. This would enable me to scribble something down even on days when my mind was clumsy with tiredness.

I was only moderately optimistic about being able to successfully complete the challenge, but it proved to be a lot easier and more rewarding than I had expected. Having a set goal each day helped me to stay focused on that small 24-hour period of time and what I had to achieve during it. It made it easier to not be intimidated by the overall goal of writing an entire book. By the end of the 30 days, although I was only part-way through the first draft, I had built up momentum. This enabled me to continue my journey with a little more confidence. The challenge had helped me to navigate my way through what can sometimes be the most difficult terrain - the Beginning.

I had forgotten just how much I enjoy the writing process and playing with words. Sometimes as I write, the sentences flow fully formed from my pen and settle comfortably on the page without fuss. Usually however, sentences have to be pummelled and pulled, words scattered in all directions before they are overpowered and ready to take their place in the narrative. Occasionally whole paragraphs and pages refuse to bend to my will, claiming a pyrrhic victory as they are relegated to the waste paper basket.

Due to my irksome health issues, it takes longer to bring the words I am looking for to mind than it used to, and I can easily forget a train of thought if I don't write it down quickly enough. I often second-guess myself on the meanings of words I used to know with confidence, but a good dictionary and thesaurus deals effectively with that. This has actually resulted in my discovering many new and useful words along the way. Except for the times when my writing had got the better of me and sent me retreating, temporarily defeated, I would return from my travels emotionally re-charged, relaxed and content.

Discovering that I am still able to write, despite a few limitations, has not only restored my confidence in this area but also in general. I now feel motivated and confident to try other activities and see where the boundaries between "possible" and "not possible yet" are. That is the wonderful feature of having even a modest victory over self-doubt, the benefits spread to other areas of one's life.

Another bonus of my journey has been a heightened awareness and appreciation of my entire environment, due to having to be more observant of my surroundings during my study explorations.

Familiarity does not always breed contempt, despite the popular saying, but it too often reduces visibility. We stop really seeing things after a certain time, reducing them to the backdrops of our lives, thus lessening the potential richness of our environments.

My initial wanderings around my study took eight weeks, two weeks longer than De Maistre's first journey around his room. I returned home with my travel journal still in its rough first draft stage. It would take many more months before the jumble of ideas and musings would be moulded into any coherent shape. Unlike some of my previous jaunts, this trip hasn't been dramatically life-changing but it has certainly been life-enhancing, and isn't that what we usually ask of our journeys, however and wherever we go?

# ACKNOWLEDGEMENTS

I would like to say a big thank you to Mum, Dad, Wendy, David and Ben for their constant encouragement and invaluable editorial help. It is deeply appreciated. Without my family's astute observations and suggestions along the way, this book would have been a misshapen shadow of its final incarnation.

I would also like to thank Benita for her encouragement throughout, and thanks too, to Heather and Valerie for their very helpful insights.

I have been fortunate to have had two very creative people, Wendy Barrett (cover photos), and Heather Leane (cover design and interior formatting), working on my book's design. Thank you both for getting my manuscript suitably dressed and ready to make its public debut. More of Wendy's and Heather's creative works can be found on their respective websites:

wendybarrettpainting.blogspot.com.au
www.sunbeambooks.com